D1480399

Elementary Teacher's Complete Handbook of Music Activities

Elementary Teacher's Complete Handbook of Music Activities

Nancy E. Forquer

Parker Publishing Company, Inc., West Nyack, N.Y.

© 1979 by

Parker Publishing Company, Inc.

West Nyack, New York

Library of Congress Cataloging in Publication

Forquer, Nancy E
  Elementary teacher's complete handbook of music
activities.

  Includes index.
  1.1. Music—Manuals, textbooks, etc. 2. Music—
Instruction and study—Juvenile.
MT10.F777   372.8'7'044   79-14154
ISBN 0-13-260703-4

  Printed in the United States of America

In memory of my mother, Frances Isabel Jackson

What This Book Will Do for You

Here is a resource book for elementary teachers that is complete, concise, and easy to use. Every aspect of music is covered with an enormous number of musical activities in each area. These activities have been used in elementary music classrooms and found to be effective teaching tools. This handbook is a vast collection of musical activities that will provide a music program that is varied, exciting to the students, and thorough in teaching specific skills and concepts.

Approximately two hundred activities have been used, evaluated, and compiled for you to incorporate into your music program. They are arranged in sections that make it easy for you to find and use:

The *Listening* section deals with *ear training, recordings, and literature*, and *timbre*. There are games, creative activities, listening guides and charts that make it easy for you to lead your students in satisfying and meaningful listening experiences.

The *Rhythm and Movement* section deals with rhythms, notation, dance, and creative movement. Again activities like "Rhythm Dice," "Pop Music and Beat," and "Rhythm Relay" are appealing to the students as well as effective teaching tools.

The section on *Creativity* guides you in that difficult task of leading students to use their full potential of creative ability. Simple kindergarten activities such as movement to music and playing simple accompaniments is gradually expanded to writing music using precise compositional techniques, improvising difficult accompaniments, and creating detailed choreographies.

Singing and Playing Skills are developed through activities in Sight Reading, Tone Matching, and Phrasing like "Tone Matching Game," "Playing with Numbers," and "Card Phrasing." They develop the students' skills gradually in many satisfying experiences.

The final section, *Theory*, *Terms*, *Games*, and *Composers* includes innovative techniques and games to expand the students' knowledge in these areas. They are activities that make drill, memorization and learning facts fun through games like "Musical Riddles" and "Hidden Word Puzzles."

The musical activities are enhanced by a Sequence Chart that will assure you have a complete and well-balanced music program each year. These new ideas will give a "lift" to the music program and make every day a new and exciting adventure for the students. In addition there are modern approaches to individualization including learning centers, learning packets, and extracurricular activities that will assure every student achieves his maximum potential and has a meaningful experience in music. These are activities and experiences that keep the students interested and excited about music to avoid discipline problems that often make teaching difficult. Objectives, step-by-step procedures, and evaluations are provided that tell you what to expect and how to judge when students are ready for advancement.

In this day of accountability, minimum standards in learning, and tests in order to receive a diploma, it is imperative that the music programs meet high standards. The music classroom is not a baby-sitting service where the classroom teachers take a break. It is no longer a place where the kids just go to "sing." The music classroom is a learning center of knowledge, skills, and attitudes. With schools in financial difficulty it is too often the music programs that are being cut. Music teachers must meet this challenge and fill their programs with substance and excitment so they will be supported by students, parents, school boards—the entire community. This book offers such a program.

Nancy E. Forquer

ACKNOWLEDGEMENTS

The author would like to express her deep appreciation to Mrs. Claudine Terry for her guidance and training; to Dr. Richard Weerts for his valuable help and encouragement in the completion of this book; and to her husband, Randy, whose patience and understanding made the preparation of this book possible.

Table of Contents

11

Guessing Game. Sound Story. Instrumental Accompaniments. Desk Sounds. Tape Recorder Timbre. Listing Sounds. Sounds Around. Instrumental Families. Constructing Instruments. Matching Sounds. Identification of Instruments. What's the Instrument?

Names in Rhythm. Name Notation. Rhythm Game. Phrase Notation. Moving to Music. Rhythm Identification. Duple and Triple Meter. Beat and Melodic Rhythm. Action Songs. Rhythm Detectives. Rhythm Diagrams. Conducting Songs. Memory Rhythm Notation. Rhythm Bouncing Ball. Thinking the Beat. Polyrhythms. Syncopation Detective. Syncopated and Unsyncopated Rhythms. "Pop" Music and Beat. Creating Dances. Rhythm Charts. Accents. Note Value Charts. Rhythm Cards. Mathematical Rhythm. Clapping Rhythm Patterns. Rhythm Gameboard and Cards. Rhythm Beat. Rhythm Baseball. Rhythm Dice. Rhythm Relay.

Space Music. Singing Puppets. Singing a Story. Composing Endings to Songs. Composition from a Design. Creating Pentatonic Songs. Creating a Major Composition. Creating an Oriental Accompaniment. Creating a Melody on the Recorder. Dramatizing a Story. Creating a Dance. Setting a Poem to Music. Creating Haiku Poetry. Creating a Twelve Tone Composition. Creativity with Form.

Preparing for Music Reading. Melodic Hand Movement. Drawing Picture Melodies. Playing Melodic Diagrams. Reading Music with Pictures. Reading Line Notation. Verbal Note Values. Rhythm Flash Cards. Clapping Numbers. Choosing Rhythm Patterns. Reading from a Two Line Staff. Methods of Sight Reading. Sight Reading Game. Reading from Treble and Bass Clef. Rhythm Match. Sight Reading Mystery. Procedures for Sight Reading.

Contents

Learning Activities Index

Learning Activities Index

Sequence Chart and Daily Schedule

In order to be certain that every facet of music is given adequate consideration, the teacher should develop a sequence chart and follow it faithfully. This sequence chart should not merely list large categories to be covered, but it should also be detailed in presenting definite learnings and concepts to be achieved in various grade levels.

When making daily lesson plans the teacher should refer to the sequence chart to discover which learnings have not been presented, which ones need reinforcement, and which concepts have been mastered by the students. (Even the "mastered" concepts should be reviewed). Various activities from the Activities Section may then be selected to teach these skills and concepts from the sequence chart.

In order to accomplish everything in the chart during the school year, the teacher must present or review several learnings during one class period. Class sessions can be divided into three parts for the purpose of presenting many activities in one class session, thus making the most effective use of time.

DAILY SCHEDULE

1. *Opening* (Five to Ten Minutes)—Music reading, Rhythms, Notes on board, Sight reading book, Kodaly charts, Mystery tune, or other opening exercises.

2. *New Learning* (Ten to Twenty Minutes)—New song, New concept or skill, or Review of old concept in a new situation.

3. *Something Fun* (Five to Ten Minutes)—Use instruments, Old song that students like, Choose songs, Listen to records, Dance, or Other activities that students enjoy.

Although the sequence chart provided in this book is very complete, teachers may differ on learnings that they expect in various grade levels and personalized charts can be developed by each teacher. Recommendations of the junior high choral, band and orchestra teachers should be considered when developing a sequence chart.

The sequence chart should be made with projected learnings included for all the grade levels, even though the teacher may be building the music program and all students may need to start with the learnings in the second or third grade level of the sequence chart. The first grade students can start on the correct level of the sequence chart, but the second through sixth grade students may need to start with learnings at lower grade levels than the grade they are in. This can be done as long as the activities selected to teach the concepts are suited to the maturity level of that particular grade. The music teacher must discover where the students are and begin at that point, gradually advancing the upper grade students to the correct grade level on the sequence chart. Consequently grades four, five and six may be working on the grade four level of the sequence chart. A music program cannot be developed in one year. It may take several years for each grade to be working with the concepts and learnings presented on their section of the sequence chart. Patience, constant referral to the sequence chart, and application of varied activities for the teaching of new concepts and reinforcement of those skills will provide a music program that is complete and fun for the students.

GRADE ONE

Creativity

Interpret music through creative movement and dance.
Dramatize stories.

Create new words to old songs.
Create melodies on the bells.
Create rhythmic accompaniments.
Improvise pentatonic patterns.
Create introductions and codas to songs.
Create songs in basic musical forms (ABA, AA, ABC).

Listening

Distinguish soft, loud, step, skip, long, short, fast, slow, up, down, beat, happy, sad, some instruments, high, low, even, uneven, meter (Two's and Three's).

Instruments—Recognize by sight and sound the tambourine, woodblock, triangle, harp, French horn, piano, drums, and flute.

Assign letters for form (AA, ABA).

Recognize music from different countries and cultures (China and American Indian).

Categorize instruments by low and high pitch.

Divide rhythm instruments into groups (clicking, ringing, thumping).

Movement

Move to music—walk, run, skip, hop, jump, slide, gallop.

Interpret mood, feeling, and rhythm in recordings by movement.

Sing and move to music at the same time.

Recognize phrases and perform various actions for different phrases.

Sing many action songs.

Playing Skills

Play the C scale on the bells.

Play easy patterns on the bells.

Play the autoharp, with some students pushing the buttons and others strumming as the teacher conducts.

Chord on the bells.

Play pentatonic accompaniments (improvised patterns) with songs.

Choose rhythm instruments appropriate for the mood and character of songs.

Play ostinato patterns on the bells.
Play Orff instrumental accompaniments.
Create melodies on the bells.
Play simple rhythmic patterns.
Categorize instruments by low and high pitch.
Recognize and play patterns going up, down by step, or skip
and repeated pitches.

Rhythm

Know and read Kodaly rhythms:

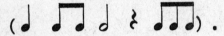

Echo all rhythmic patterns.
Know the difference between beat and rhythm.
Identify even and uneven rhythmic patterns.
Identify meter in two's or three's.
Recognize fast and slow tempo.

Singing and Music Reading

Know many rote songs.
Be able to match pitches.
Sing three note patterns alone.
Read numbers one, three, five, and six.
Assign letters for form (AA, ABA).
Divide songs into phrases.
Recognize repeat sign.
Sing ostinato patterns.
Sing and recognize music from different countries (Chinese,
Oriental, Indian).
Sight read from the first Mary Helen Richards Chart.
Sing songs individually.
Show with hands the melodic direction of songs.
Sing with expression (slow, fast, loud, soft, continuous
phrases).
Encourage a light sound instead of loud singing with an open
throat.
Recognize and sing up, down, step, skip, and repeated
pitches.

Follow songs in books (know how many staffs are in the song).
Locate certain types of notes (whole, half, quarter, or eighth) on the different staffs.
Sing many action songs.

GRADE TWO

Creativity

Continue using skills and knowledge acquired in First Grade.
Create songs, making up phrases on the bells to a line of original poetry (Haiku).
Create pentatonic songs and accompaniments.
Create larger compositions using multiple sounds (such as a simple melody with rhythmic accompaniment).
Use creative physical response to music.
Create percussion scores and play compositions.

Listening

Continue using skills and knowledge acquired in the First Grade.
Listen for musical elements (tempo, dynamics, timbre, mood, beat) and use correct terms.
Instrument recognition by sight and sound (add clarinet, oboe, tuba, and trumpet).
Recognize more complicated forms (ABACA, ABCA, ABCD).
Recognize phrases by listening.
Continue ear training process to recognize rhythms and melodic direction.

Movement

Continue using skills and knowledge acquired in First Grade.
Perform movements together, such as running and walking (clap running rhythm and step walking rhythm).
Put the beat in the feet and the melodic rhythm in the hands simultaneously.
Interpret longer creative dance movements.
Move to the music using a "step-clap, step-clap" sequence.

Use singing games, simple folk dances, and free interpretation.

Plan dance movements to reflect the form of the music.

Playing Skills

Continue using skills and knowledge acquired in First Grade.

Improvise melodies on the bells.

Play the C, F, and G scales on the bells.

Play chords on the autoharp (or bells). Chord with the teacher directing.

Play a pentatonic song and accompaniment.

Play accompaniments on Orff instruments (use combinations of three or four instruments).

Read rhythms from the chalkboard using rhythm instruments.

Select instruments for accompaniments which are expressively appropriate.

Experiment with many kinds of instrumental and natural sounds.

Rhythm

Continue using skills and knowledge acquired in First Grade.

Recognize and read the following rhythms using the "Kodaly" method:

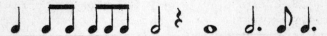

Read rhythms of songs directly from books.

Conduct in 2/4, 3/4, and 4/4 time.

Read and perform rhythmic compositions, using rhythm instruments.

Take rhythm dictation.

Groups perform two and three different rhythms simultaneously.

Singing and Music Reading

Continue using skills and knowledge acquired in First Grade.

Study the printed page—staff, time signature, sharps, flats, dynamic markings (p, f, mp, mf), repeat signs, fermata, accent, crescendo, decrescendo.

Read rhythms of songs from textbook.

Improve ability to match pitch and increase range.

Sing three-and four-note melodic patterns alone.

Know all the numbers for sight reading (one through eight) and read simple patterns without difficult skips.

Sing rounds and ostinato patterns.

Begin singing in thirds.

Sing simple two-part songs and partner songs.

Complete the second Mary Helen Richards Chart.

Sing verses of songs as solos and duets.

Realize the importance of singing clearly and accurately.

Sing complete phrases.

Be aware of melodic direction on the printed page.

GRADE THREE

Creativity

Continue using skills and knowledge acquired in previous grades.

Create poems, new words to old songs, music in various forms, ostinato patterns and accompaniments.

Create codas, interludes, and introductions.

Create dance routines.

Create notated rhythmic rounds and play them.

Notate created melodies using numbers or syllables.

Consider accent groupings and rhythmic relationships in planning dance movements.

Become aware of repetition and contrast in creative efforts.

Use expressive elements (tempo, dynamics, mood, instrumentation) in creative efforts.

Listening

Continue using skills and knowledge developed in previous grades.

Listen to music and distinguish elements (tempo, dynamics, form, melody, rhythm, mood, timbre) and use correct musical terms.

Be more aware of themes and their development.

Recognize all the instruments of the orchestra by sight and sound.

Distinguish music from other countries (Oriental, Indian, African, Spanish, Jamaican).

Determine appropriate chord accompaniments.

Determine ways in which contrasts are achieved melodically, rhythmically, and instrumentally.

Distinguish major, minor, chromatic and pentatonic scale patterns.

Begin intervalic ear training.

Take more complicated rhythmic dictation.

Movement

Continue using skills and knowledge developed in previous grades.

Use more sophisticated creative dance movements to records.

Dance to pop records—develop uninhibited ability to move to the music.

Perform simple square dances.

Consider melodic contour in planning dance movements.

Consider accent groupings and rhythmic relationships in planning dance movements.

Playing Skills

Continue using skills and knowledge developed in previous grades.

Learn to write and play all of the major scales by use of whole and half steps (WWHWWWH).

Play rhythmic rounds and canons.

Play the autoharp with one student pointing to the music and the other person strumming and chording.

Play Orff instruments (or other melodic and rhythmic instruments).

Know families of instruments and the principal instruments contained in each family by sight and sound.

Rhythm

> Continue using skills and knowledge developed in previous grades.
>
> Read all Kodaly rhythms from the chalkboard, charts, and in printed music.
>
> Read more complicated rhythms from music books using syncopation.
>
> Conduct in 2/4, 3/4, 4/4, and 6/8 time.
>
> Reproduce all rhythmic patterns in songs.
>
> Become aware of irregular meter (5/4, 7/4).
>
> Become aware of shifting meter.

Singing and Music Reading

> Continue using skills and knowledge developed in previous grades.
>
> Read more complicated rhythms and melodic patterns from books.
>
> Continue the study of the printed music following directions on the printed page. (Add various tempo and dynamic markings along with repeat signs).
>
> Match pitch and reproduce difficult melodic patterns.
>
> Sing five and six note melodic patterns alone.
>
> Begin regular sequential sight reading series.
>
> Read familiar songs and try to guess what they are.
>
> Sing ostinato patterns, rounds, counter-melodies, descants, sing in thirds, partner songs, and songs in two parts containing two staffs.
>
> Strive for improved tone quality and diction.
>
> Use knowledge of repetition and contrast to help learn new songs when scanning the music for the first time.
>
> Be aware of key signatures.

GRADE FOUR

Creativity

> Continue using skills and knowledge developed in previous grades.
>
> Create music using notation (staffs, clefs, rhythms, measures, time signatures, and notes).

Create songs in specific forms.

Create dance movements to pop records and more serious listening examples.

Use altered tones (sharps and flats) in original compositions.

Experiment with electronic sound compositions.

Create compositions using body sounds, nature sounds, or recorded sounds.

Listening

Continue using skills and knowledge developed in previous grades.

Continue identifying all musical elements in listening examples.

Concentrate on musical themes and their development.

Study various forms in relation to listening examples.

Start studying music history and classifying listening examples into periods (use a time line).

Study composers of listening examples.

Review instruments (and families of instruments) by sight and sound and learn their position in the orchestra.

Take dictation of simple melodic and rhythmic patterns.

Movement

Continue using skills and knowledge developed in previous grades.

Use rock and roll dance forms.

Perform more difficult square dances.

Learn the Hora, waltz, slow dances, and line dances.

Learn many dances typical of other countries and times.

Create movements for songs considering melody, rhythm, form, dynamics, and mood of the music.

Playing Skills

Continue using skills and knowledge developed in previous grades.

Begin music reading with recorders.

Use piano, bells, marimbas, and other melodic intruments to develop sight reading skills.

Be able to write scales by use of whole and half steps and then find the I, IV, and V chords.

```
I       IV V
C D E F G A B C
E       A   B
G       C   D
```

Write the scales and chords on staff paper and play them on keyboard instruments.

Read and play longer melodic patterns.

Play the autoharp without the aid of other students or of the teacher's pointing.

Play more difficult accompaniments.

Rhythm

Continue using skills and knowledge developed in previous grades.

Transfer from Kodaly system of rhythms to regular names and note values.

Study note values (clap, write, and use in music reading).

Know and use all rhythmic values, including notes and rests.

Fill in measures with counts in various time signatures.

Singing and Music Reading

Continue using skills and knowledge developed in previous grades.

Learn note names of the treble clef and begin written theory papers.

Fill in work sheets on music theory.

Sight read from sight reading series.

Begin two-part sight reading.

Begin using easy sheet music in two parts.

Develop good singing techniques (and tone qualities) with a wide range.

GRADE FIVE
Creativity

Continue using skills and knowledge developed in previous grades.

Create songs within a harmonic framework.

Create descants to go with songs and remain in the harmonic framework of the song.

Notate original songs filling expression markings.

Create a theme and variation.

Listening

Continue using skills and knowledge developed in previous grades.

Use ear to choose major and minor chords to accompany songs.

Listen to recordings and study the historical significance of the music and the composers.

Do extensive studies on Jazz and Electronic music.

Study theme and variation and sonata allegro forms in detail.

Study tension, release, and climax in music as well as musical elements in listening examples.

Take more complicated dictation of melodic and rhythmic patterns.

Movement

Continue using skills and knowledge developed in previous grades.

Perform more difficult dances.

Have students demonstrate the current popular dances for the class to learn.

Create movements to music to perform for programs.

Learn dances from other times and countries (waltz, polka, minuet, mazurka, Mexican Hat Dance, Hora, schottische, cha-cha, twist, jitterbug).

Playing Skills

Continue using skills and knowledge developed in previous grades.

Play the autoharp individually, using more chord changes.

Read simple songs on keyboard instruments.

Play duets together, using various combinations of rhythmic and melodic instruments.

Study instruments from other countries and perform on them if possible.

Study sound production and make instruments (stringed, percussion, and wind instruments).

Work with chromatic, twelve tone, and whole tone scales.

Rhythm

Continue using skills and knowledge developed in previous grades.

Read all rhythms by clapping and playing them on percussion instruments.

Use all rhythms to create songs.

Divide given rhythms into measures.

Work with rhythms on staff paper, using all time signatures.

Study polyrhythms and be able to perform them.

Singing and Music Reading

Continue using skills and knowledge developed in previous grades.

Continue work sheets on note values, note names, and basic harmonic theory.

Advance sight reading program to more difficult two-part songs.

Vocal chord, using the I, IV, and V chords.

Continue singing two-part songs and advance to simple three-part songs.

Apply understanding of major scale structure to the printed score.

GRADE SIX

Creativity

Continue using skills and knowledge developed in previous grades.

Study works by composers and try to incorporate compositional techniques into original compositions (sequence, rhythmic patterns, melodic patterns, repetition, form, unity, variety, tension, release, and climax).

Create songs in harmonic framework using I, ii, iii, IV, V, vi, and vii° cords. Always write compositions on the staff and be able to play them.

Create compositions using tone rows.

Work with bitonality and polytonality.

Create original compositions in various styles and forms.

Listening

Continue using skills and knowledge developed in previous grades.

Use acquired knowledge to work individually researching history and composers of compositions, discovering and filling in work-sheet questions concerning the elements of music.

Study contrapuntal techniques.

Study and listen to all forms (opera, oratorio, mass, ballet, symphony, quartet, sonata allegro, song forms, waltzes, nocturnes, preludes, mazurkas, theme and variations, rondos, tone poem, twelve tone music, sonata, solo, jazz, minuet, canzona, fugue, madrigal, dance suite).

Movement

Continue using skills and knowledge developed in previous grades.

Perform large dance productions and musicals.

Join in extra-curricular activities available in the dance medium.

Participate in drill teams and march squads supporting local ball teams.

Playing Skills

Continue using skills and knowledge developed in previous grades.

Play simple melodies on all of the keyboard instruments and recorder.

Begin ukelele and extra-curricular guitar lessons.

Use acquired knowledge to work individually without the teacher's assistance.

Perform duets, trios, and quartets using combinations of melodic and rhythmic instruments.

Rhythm

Continue using skills and knowledge developed in previous grades.

Read all rhythms from the chalkboard, charts and books.

Read rhythms and play them on instruments.

Use rhythms correctly in notating rhythmic compositions.

Fill in advanced work sheets concerning rhythms.

Singing and Music Reading

Continue using skills and knowledge developed in previous grades.

Learn to adjust to changing voices.

Read music in two and three parts.

Observe tempo and dynamic markings and sing with expression when reading music.

Continue advanced theory work sheets on rhythm, harmony, forms, and terms.

Continue advanced sight reading series.

Sing more difficult two and three part songs.

Sing music of better quality in order to prepare students for the junior high choral groups.

Have an extra-curricular chorus available for interested students.

Develop sensitivity to melodic line and balance when singing.

Develop the qualities of musical interpretation and production.

Chapter 1

Listening Activities for Ear Training

Activities in this section will deal with methods and techniques designed to improve the student's ability to distinguish rhythms, tonal memory, and melodic recognition. Short activities should be performed daily in order to strengthen the student's concepts and skills in these areas.

ECHO CLAPPING

Students will improve their listening skills by echo clapping.

Procedure

The teacher must clap a rhythmic pattern, then pause while students echo the same pattern. There should be no hesitation by students so that the beat is not lost. Simple patterns may be used with beginning students and more difficult patterns with syncopation and intricate rhythms used for advanced students.

Evaluation

The teacher must evaluate students as they perform. If students lose the beat or are not together the teacher should repeat the rhythm. As students master simple rhythmic patterns the teacher should try new and more difficult rhythms.

INSTRUMENT DIRECTIONS

Students will improve their listening ability by walking when a musical instrument (other than a drum) is played and standing still and clapping when the drum is played.

Procedure

A leader is chosen and instructed to play a musical instrument for several seconds, then switch to the drum. This is repeated several times while the remaining students walk to the beat when the musical instrument is played and stand still and clap when the drum is played. After one minute the leader may choose another student to take his place and the game continues.

Evaluation

Students must listen in order to stay with the beat (as well as listen to the timbre of the sound) and change their action to correspond. If a student is having difficulty the teacher may walk beside him or ask him to stand beside a student who has accomplished the skill. If many students are having diffuculty the teacher should go back and review the beat and moving with the beat.

ENDING NOTES

Students will improve their listening skills by indicating which note ends the song.

Procedure

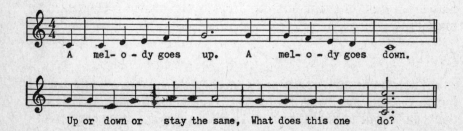

Students and the teacher should sing the preceding song together except for the last note. The teacher should sing the last note alone as the students listen. Students respond to the ending note by reaching in the air if it is the third space C, standing at attention if it is the second line G or by touching the floor if it is the middle C. Those who are wrong may drop out or the teacher may wish to start the game again.

Evaluation

The teacher may easily see which students are able to detect the final pitch by their movement. If students are watching to see how others are responding before making a decision, the teacher may wish to have the students close their eyes as they play the game. Individual help may be needed by certain students repeating this and other games determining final pitches. Many similar singing games should be used in a primary ear training program.

DRUM RHYTHMS

Students will improve their listening skills by responding to rhythms played on a drum.

Procedure

The teacher (or a student selected by the teacher) should play various rhythm patterns on a drum:

Students should respond to the correct rhythm by running, walking, skipping, or hopping. Between each set of rhythms a pause should occur before a different pattern begins. After students have mastered these movements with the proper pauses, the teacher may play patterns and proceed without pausing.

Evaluation

The teacher may observe students to see if they are responding to the rhythms with the correct movement. Most of the students will respond correctly, and those who respond incorrectly will

quickly change when seeing others doing a different motion. After
playing the rhythm a few seconds the teacher may call out the
correct motion.

INTERPRETATION WITH BODY MOVEMENT

Students will improve their listening skills by interpreting
music with body movement.

Procedure

The teacher should choose songs that suggest various moods
or movements. These may include happy, sad, light excited moods;
or walking, marching, hopping, skipping movements. Students
should listen and respond to the music by using body movement.
Short examples of various songs may be played with pauses between so that students may change movements several times.

Evaluation

Each student's interpretation of the music should be unique.
There will be no "correct" response. However, the teacher may
wish to bring attention to a particular interpretation by saying,
"Look at Mary. She is moving very slowly like the music." or "I
like the way Bob is using his whole body to show how the music
goes."

HIGH LIMBER, LOW STIFF

Students will improve their concept of high and low by standing stiff when a low melody is played and becoming limber when a
high melody is played.

Procedure

The teacher should give students several examples of high and
low pitches by playing them on the piano, bells, guitar, or other
melodic instruments. Students should then find a place in the room
where there is adequate space to move. If the teacher plays a low

melody students should stand stiff. They should become limber if a high melody is played.

Evaluation

As the teacher observes students she (he) will be able to see how many have grasped the concept of high and low. Many experiences may be needed for students to understand and respond correctly. Different instruments should be used to acquaint students with timbres and high and low sounds on many instruments.

SCALE MOVEMENT

Students will improve their concept of descending melody by bending lower for each note of the scale.

Procedure

Students should listen to several descending scale passages and discuss possible movements to show the direction of the melody. The teacher may use a suggested movement given by the class or instruct students to gradually move to the floor from a standing position. As various descending scales are played students should move with the music.

Evaluation

At first students may move too slowly (not reaching the floor) or too quickly (reaching the floor before the the scale is completed). Several attempts may be made before students are able to regulate their body movements with the scale passage. After students have mastered the descending scale, the teacher may introduce ascending passages (or descending and ascending thirds) emphasizing movement by steps or skips.

LIONS AND BIRDS

Students will improve their listening skills and concept of high and low by moving as a lion or bird.

Procedure

Students should listen to the following:

An explanation should be given by the teacher stating that Example Number One is the "Lions" and Example Number Two is the "Birds." The Lions are to walk only when they hear Example Number One and the birds pretend to fly when they hear Example Number Two. The teacher may instruct students to go anywhere in the forest (but not to bump into the other lions or birds). As the teacher plays either example one or two, the correct group should move through the forest.

Evaluation

The teacher must watch students to see that the correct group is moving. If some students are having difficulty she may call out the correct name—"Lions" or "Birds." Appropriate music for other examples of high and low might include elephants for low, mice for high, or trucks for low and cars for high.

LISTEN TO THE LEADER

Students will improve their listening skills by repeating a musical example played by the leader.

Procedure

A leader should be chosen and everyone should close their eyes except the leader. A number of rhythm instruments should be available to the leader. As everyone's eyes are closed the leader should select an instrument and play beats fast or slow and loud or soft. As eyes are opened the leader should choose someone to repeat what he played on the correct instrument. If the student is correct he becomes the leader and the game continues. If not, the old leader plays another example and should select a new student to play the example.

Evaluation

If students are not able to repeat the correct example, the teacher may limit the choice of instruments to two and review dynamics and tempo. Other instruments may be added and simple rhythmic patterns attempted as the students improve.

BEAT WITH MOTIONS

Students will improve their listening skills and concept of beat by keeping the beat with different motions.

Procedure

Several recordings should be selected with various tempos, but all should have a steady beat that is easy to follow. Students need many experiences keeping the beat by clapping, stamping, patting knees, and snapping. A leader may be chosen and students should follow the leader by keeping the beat with their hands and clapping on the head, shoulders, knees or the floor.

Evaluation

Students who have considerable difficulty with this exercise may have certain learning disabilities and a recommendation to the proper school official may be necessary. Some students in the first or second grade may have difficulty with the skill but still have no particular learning disability. Repetition and review will normally solve this problem.

VERBALIZATION OF HIGH AND LOW

Students will improve their concept of high and low by verbalizing whether sounds are high or low.

Procedure

The teacher should have melodic instruments (such as piano, guitar, xylophone, or recorder) in a place where the students cannot see them. As two tones are played on a particular melodic instrument the students should be able to tell which tone was higher or lower. After students are able to hear the difference between two tones, the teacher may want to show the students that smaller things produce higher pitch and larger things produce lower sounds. This would be easily shown by using resonator bells or the strings on a piano or autoharp.

Evaluation

After several sessions of verbalizing, the teacher may wish to give a written quiz to see which students have the concept and which ones need to work on it.

CREATIVE ECHO

Students will improve their listening skills by listening to a rhythmic pattern and answering it creatively.

Procedure

After students have had many experiences echoing rhythm patterns they may proceed to this activity; that is, where a child claps a rhythm pattern to be answered creatively.

It is important that the beat is not lost during the activity.[1]

Evaluation

At first students will find it difficult to listen to a pattern and quickly improvise another. It may be necessary to practice clapping a written exercise (as shown above) and then proceed to the improvisation.

---

[1]Robert Evans Nye and Vernice Trousdale Nye, *Essentials of Teaching Elementary School Music* (Englewood Cliffs: Prentice Hall, 1974), p. 76.

CANON ECHOES

Students will improve their listening ability by echoing rhythms in canon form.

Procedure

The teacher should clap a continuous rhythmic pattern in a specific meter and tempo. Students should remember what was clapped and repeat it later while at the same time hearing and remembering what the leader is doing.[2]

Evaluation

This activity is a continuation of simple echo clapping beginning in first grade and advancing to the upper grade levels. Encouragement and praise should be given as often as possible since many experiences will be needed before students are successful at echoing in canon form.

INSTRUMENTAL DIRECTIONS

Students will improve their listening skills by listening to instruments and moving in assigned directions.

Procedure

Five instruments must be selected and assigned specific directions, (forward-bell, backward-sticks, right-tambourine, left-drum, and turn-maraca). Students then close their eyes and follow directions by listening to the instrument playing and moving in that direction. A large area will be needed and the teacher must be careful to play certain instruments so that students can move without obstruction.

---

[2]Nye, op. cit., p. 105.

Evaluation

Students should all be moving in the same direction together. This activity may be used as a game with students dropping out as they move in the wrong direction. In this way the teacher can easily see which students need more practice.

RHYTHM TUNE DETECTIVE

Students will improve their listening skills by identifying tunes from their melodic rhythm.

Procedure

A list of songs should be written on the board so that the leader may choose one and clap the melodic rhythm. As a rhythm is clapped students should try to identify the song. The first student to name the song becomes the leader and the game continues.

Evaluation

The teacher may watch to see which students are able to identify songs correctly. A written test may be given later for a more accurate evaluation.

MATCHING BELL TONES

Students will improve their listening skills by matching a pitch played on a recorder.

Procedure

The teacher should prepare a tape using a set of resonator bells and sounding a specific pitch for fifteen seconds. After a pause the name of the pitch is given and a new one is sounded for another fifteen seconds. Students should use the tape recorder along with a set of resonator bells to match the pitch being sounded. Once they have found the pitch they play for the remain-

der of the fifteen seconds and then listen as the note name is called
to see if they were correct. The activity then continues to the next
note.[3]

Evaluation

This activity may be set up outside the classroom with students individually leaving the room and proceeding through the
tape. If this is the case, the students evaluate themselves as the
note name is given on the recorder.

DICTATION GAME

Students will improve their listening skills by playing a dictation game.

Procedure

This game may be played by relay teams at the board, or the
entire class using paper at their desks. The teacher plays a
rhythmic pattern and students attempt to write it down. Those
who miss must drop out of the game until one person remains.

Evaluation

The teacher may evaluate by noticing which students drop out
early and which students remain to the end. After students have
dropped out they may move to another area in the room and still
try to notate the rhythmic patterns. In this way the learning continues even with students who have missed rhythms early in the
game.

MUSIC DICTATION

Students will improve their music listening skills by taking
music dictation.

---

[3]Eugene L. Beenk, *Music Teacher's Resource Manual* (Iowa, Music Educator Aids,
1974), p. 7. contributed by Mr. Harold Dunn.

Procedure

Melodic dictation may begin by having students draw pictures of a melody with their hands in the air or using paper at their desks.

If the melodies go up, hands should rise. If the melody goes down hands are lowered, or if the melody stays on the same note, hands remain on the same level. The same is done on paper. Lines go up, down, or stay the same according to the melody.

The next step would be rhythmic dictation using simple rhythms and advancing to more complicated patterns. Actual dictation using a staff and rhythms should begin by using two or three notes. As students are able to handle more notes and more difficult rhythms, the teacher should gradually make the dictation more complicated.

Evaluation

The teacher should collect the papers and examine them carefully. If students are able to take the dictation correctly, more difficult songs should be used. If most of the students are not able to record the music on paper, easier material and review may be necessary.

Chapter 2

Listening Activities Using Musical Recordings

Activities in this section will deal with methods and techniques designed to improve the student's ability to listen to musical recordings. The student's appreciation of the music will be expanded by guidance and practice in listening, responding to the music, and identifying musical elements.

INDIAN MUSIC

Students will improve their listening skills and concept of American Indian music by making Indian costumes and dancing in a circle.

Procedure

After a discussion of Indian customs, dress, dances, and songs an Indian song or recording should be chosen. The students may make head bands and costumes at home, in music, or in art class. As they wear their costumes they should stand in a circle keeping the beat by walking and hopping. They may wish to use maracas, bells, woodblocks, or other appropriate rhythm instruments as they dance. They could use various rhythm patterns as follows:

Evaluation

Most of the students will be able to perform this activity, but the teacher should be alert for those having difficulty and provide additional activities of this type. If the problem is severe the teacher may wish to consult the classroom teacher, the physical education teacher, or the school nurse.

LISTENING MUSIC PUPPETS

Students will improve their listening skills by pretending to be puppets and moving to the music.

Procedure

Students should experiment and discuss how puppets move by using hand puppets and puppets on a string. After this discussion a record that has a definite beat, suggests a certain movement, or has contrasting movement should be played. Students should first listen to the record and suggest types of movements that might be appropriate. The second time the record is played students should pretend that they are puppets and move to the music.

Evaluation

Since there is no "right" or "wrong" way to do this activity the teacher should not evaluate in the usual sense. This activity should help students become more relaxed with movement, help them to react to the music and help them to become less inhibited. The teacher should observe and provide other activities of this type until the class is comfortable in this situation.

MOVEMENT WITH JAPANESE FANS

Students will improve their listening skills and concept of Oriental music by moving with Japanese fans.

Procedure

Pictures and film strips may be presented of Japanese dancers with fans to show the gracefulness of the dancers so that students can imitate their movements. The students may attempt to move with their fans as they listen to the recording the first time, or listen through the recording and then move while using their fans. Fans may be made from construction paper, or a joint effort of the art and music teachers could provide more elaborate fans.

Evaluation

Comments should be made to the students, such as:
"Look at Johnny. His movements are very graceful."
"Sue, make your movements smoother."
"Try going in a circle with your hands over your head and bend down as you do it."
Such suggestions will encourage experimentation, and stiff movements can be noticed and improved.

LISTENING SPACE ADVENTURE

Students will improve their listening skills by pretending the music is pulling them into space.

Procedure

A slow, light, airy composition would be a good selection for this activity rather than music that is fast and harsh with a driving rhythm. After the selection has been heard once, the teacher should ask students to line up against the wall. As the record is played again students should let the music pull them into space.

Evaluation

The success of such an activity depends on the student's ability to let the music penetrate his body and move him into space. This will take concentration and the ability to react to the music. Each student will have a different interpretation of the music and the teacher should encourage shy and inhibited students to join in the group. This type of activity should be started at an early age and continued in the upper grades. Other listening adventures include pretending to be a bouncing ball, or using balloons or scarves to move to the music.

MUSICAL THEMES

Students will improve their listening skills by singing, playing, and recognizing the theme of a recording.

Procedure

When listening to music the teacher may acquaint the students with the theme by playing it on the piano or bells. If it is not too difficult the students may play the entire theme or parts of it themselves. Themes that are too difficult to play may be sung, or the rhythm could be clapped. As the recording is played, students should raise their hands when they hear the theme or quietly count the number of times it appears and give the answer at the end of the recording.

Evaluation

The teacher may use this as a means of written evaluation by playing principal themes as students identify them with the correct recordings or by having students count the number of times a certain theme appears in the music. Recognition of the theme is essential in the study of form, so there should be many experiences provided for students to gain this concept.

ATTENDING A CONCERT

Students will improve their listening skills by giving reports and discussing notes of a concert to be attended.

Procedure

When planning to attend a concert, the teacher should obtain a program and any notes that may be available. If notes are not available, the teacher should devise her own by using the program and finding information about the music and composers. The students may help with the collection of this information by giving oral or written reports about the music to be performed.

Evaluation

The teacher may evaluate students by oral or written reports to be given as a class project. If the teacher has obtained notes of the performance, she may wish to lead the class in a discussion and evaluate by this means. A third method of evaluation would be to present the information and give a written test.

CONCERT SKIT

Students will improve their concept of a concert by presenting a skit of things never done at a concert.

Procedure

The teacher should lead students in a discussion of "How people should behave at a concert." Such aspects as whispering, talking, rattling, wriggling, laughing, and applauding at inappropriate times should be considered. After the discussion the class may be divided into groups and skits developed around the subject of "Behavior not acceptable at a concert." These skits may be presented to the class or to younger classes that will be attending the concert.

Evaluation

The teacher may evaluate concepts learned by observing various behaviors brought out in the skits. The final and most effective evaluation is students' behavior as they attend the concert.

PROGRAM MUSIC

Students will improve their concept of program music by listening to records and trying to guess what the composer is trying to represent.

Procedure

Several recordings can be used that depict scenes, animals, and birds. As a portion of each recording is played students should guess what the composer is trying to represent. When the desired answer is given the next recording may be played.

Evaluation

Although the composer has chosen a specific subject students should not be made to feel that their guesses are "incorrect." The teacher may reinforce this idea with such comments as "Yes, it does sound exciting like a _____, but that's not what the composer had in mind," or "That's a good answer but not the one I was looking for."

LISTENING OUTLINE

Students will improve their listening skills by following activities on a listening outline.

Procedure

This outline may be used by the teacher to lead students in discussions and activities for listening.

   I. Name of composer and title of music
        A. Facts about composer
        B. Explanation of historic elements when music was written
  II. Students discover characteristics as recording is played—tempo, mood, dynamics
 III. Students discover timbre
        A. Families and specific instruments
        B. Discussion of why composer chose particular instruments
  IV. Explanation of form
        A. Notation of themes
        B. Recognition of themes in specific form
   V. Summary
  VI. Repeated listening for oral and written explanation of musical elements and enjoyment

Evaluation

This outline will take several lessons to complete. Final evaluation may include discussions, observation, and written tests.

LISTENING SHEET

Students will improve their listening skills by filling out a listening sheet.

Procedure

The following may be used as a guide when preparing a listening work sheet.

Question	Answer
1. Does the beat go in Twos or Threes?	1. Twos Threes
2. Which beat is accented?	2. 1 2 3 4
3. Do you hear syncopation?	3. Yes No
4. Write down the repeated rhythm pattern of the bass drum	4.
5. What instrument plays the melody?	5.
6. Do you hear a soloist or a choir?	6. Solist Choir
7. Are the strings plucked or bowed?	7. Plucked Bowed
8. Name three instruments that you hear.	8.
9. Do you hear harmony in the voices?	9.
10. How many times is the chorus repeated?	10.
11. Is the first theme repeated at the end?	11. Yes No
12. Does the music have an introduction?	12. Yes No
13. Write the form of the song using ABC's.	13.
14. Choose the best word to describe the mood of the music.	14. Quiet, Excited, Dreamy

15. Is the music loudest at the beginning, middle or end?

15. Beginning   Middle   End

16. Do the dynamics change suddenly or gradually?

16. Suddenly   Gradually

17. Where is the music fastest?

17. Beginning   Middle   End

18. Mark the best answer for the tempo of the music.

18. Slow slow fast
Slow Fast Slow
Fast Slow Fast

19. Is this program or absolute music?

19. Program   Absolute

20. What does the music best describe?

20. Birds   Elephants
A Fight

Evaluation

Evaluation will result in papers being collected and scored. If students do poorly they probably need more guidance as a class project and discussion before attempting a work sheet on their own.

PREPARING A LISTENING LESSON

Students will improve their listening skills by following a listening outline.

Procedure

The following outline may be used by the teacher to make a listening work sheet or by students as they discuss a recording:

"I. List song's sections (introduction, verse, chorus; or AABB, etc.).

II. Look for repetition, contrast, and repetition with variation within and between the sections.

III. Outline instrumentation of sections.

IV. Make note of mood or intensity progression throughout the song.

V. Listen for musical quotes or style imitations of other compositions.

VI. Find obvious word paintings.

VII. Listen for clear demonstrations of common musical concepts such as tempo, meter, dynamic changes, modulations, pedal point, ostinato, etc.

VIII. Listen for points of view on social problems of the day or persistant human dilemmas—pollution, race problems, power struggle, love, etc.[4]"

Evaluation

The teacher may evaluate students by answers given during a discussion of a recording. It is important that all students enter into the discussion. It may be necessary for the teacher to draw shy students into the discussion by asking them direct questions that require an opinion instead of a definite answer. By using this method, a student must think about the recording, voice an opinion, and can be reinforced by having a "right" answer, since no answer can be wrong.

CHANGING AND IRREGULAR METER

Students will improve their listening skills by discovering songs that use changing and irregular meters.

Procedure

Students should have had many previous experiences working with meter and beat. The teacher may then play recordings where the meter changes. After students have discovered this changing

---

[4]Michael Don Bennett, *Surviving in General Music* (881 S. Cooper, Memphis, Tennessee: Pop Hits Publishing, 1974), p. 1.

meter, they may clap and discover irregular and changing meter in other selections as well as bring recordings from home.

Evaluation

The teacher may evaluate students as various recordings are played and as irregular and changing meters are discovered. This may be done in the form of a discussion, written work, or a requirement of records brought to class as examples.

CHORD CLUSTERS

Students will improve their concept of contemporary music by playing chord clusters and discussing records that use this technique.

Procedure

Students should practice playing chord clusters of four to six notes on the piano or bells. A student might use both hands at the piano, or four to six students may each choose a separate resonator bell to achieve chord clusters. Several of these may be played for different sounds and effects. The students could also write chord clusters on a staff for the teacher to play. After this, experimentation recordings containing chord clusters should be played. Students should be able to point out areas containing the chord clusters.

Evaluation

The teacher should first evaluate students by playing chord clusters among major and minor chords for the students to recognize. The teacher may then watch to see if students can play chord clusters on the piano or bells. Finally, the teacher may give a written examination to see if students are able to recognize chord clusters in recordings.

BLUE NOTES

Students will improve their concept of contemporary music by singing and discovering music that uses "blue notes."

Procedure

This activity may be included in a unit on jazz as well as a combined study of contemporary music. Students should practice singing flatted thirds, fifths, and sevenths and such songs as "Joe Turner Blues" or "Seventy-Six Highway Blues" that contain blue notes. Students should then identify blue notes in the songs they have sung and listen to recordings of jazz with blue notes.

Evaluation

The teacher may evaluate students through their discussion of blue notes and their ability to point out examples in songs. This may also be accomplished through listening and outside material that is brought into class.

ELECTRONIC AND DISTORTED SOUND

Students will improve their concept of contemporary music by creating a composition using electronic and distorted sounds.

Procedure

This activity will require certain equipment, such as, an electric guitar with an amplifier, a microphone, and a tape recorder. Various sounds should be collected on a tape recorder such as voice sounds or electronic sounds produced by a coffee pot, electric razor, television set, telephone, can opener, etc. These sounds may then be distorted by methods such as slowing down, speeding up, recording at one speed and playing at another, running the recorder backwards, and taping on top of another tape. The total composition may then be organized. Form, unity, variety, repetition, climax, and organization should be included in the composition.

Evaluation

The tape recorder will be the principal instrument of evaluation for this activity. The teacher may listen and lead students in a discussion of their creation of electronic and distorted sounds. A total sound composition should stress the elements of good compositional techniques, such as unity and variety. Finally, recordings should be obtained where electronic and distorted sound is used in twentieth century music.

CHANCE MUSIC

Students will improve their concept of contemporary music by listening to and creating a composition of chance music.

Procedure

This activity may be used as an introduction before listening to chance music. The teacher must first explain the concept of chance music and then give students an opportunity to create a composition. Some methods are as follows:

1. Use dice with letter names and write the notes that come up as the dice are thrown.

2. Draw letters from a box and write notes on the staff in that order.

3. Punch holes in a paper and lay it over the staff drawing notes in the holes.

4. Take a printed page and use only letters that can be written on the staff in correct order.

Evaluation

Since chance music cannot be "right" or "wrong" the teacher should not evaluate in the usual sense. The composition may be written and discussed by students with suggestions for improvement. After this procedure recordings may be played and a student could be asked to explain to the class how chance music is developed. This may also be done by the use of an essay question given for evaluation.

TWELVE TONE COMPOSITION

Students will improve their concept of contemporary music by listing tone rows in a twelve tone composition.

Procedure

The teacher must explain the use of an original twelve tone row, avoiding leading tones and traditional skips outlining chords. After students have had some experience creating their own tone rows they may listen to a twelve tone composition and try to notate the original row from a printed copy of the music. Examples of the original row (retrograde, inversion, or retrograde-inversion) may be found and listed. Students should have a better understanding of twelve tone music after the mechanics of their compositional technique have been explained and understood.

Evaluation

Evidence of students' understanding of how the tone row works may be gained as they mark rows in the printed music. Appreciation of this type of music may be a gradual process and the teacher must be aware of the attitudes of the class concerning twelve tone music.

Chapter 3

Listening Activities That Teach Timbre Identification

These listening activities will deal with methods and techniques designed to improve students' ability to identify and classify various timbres. Creative activities are also presented so that students may employ the knowledge acquired through the study of timbre.

SOUND EXPERIMENT

Students will improve their concept of sound by putting sugar or salt on a cymbal and watching it move.

Procedure

Students may discuss how sound is produced and then perform this experiment or the teacher may wish to perform the experiment and ask students to explain why the sugar moves. Salt or sugar should be sprinkled on a cymbal and as it is struck with a drum stick the salt (or sugar) will bounce around. Students may discuss this until they understand that vibrations cause sound and that these same vibrations cause the salt to move.

Evaluation

The teacher may evaluate students by listening to their discussions about sound. It may be necessary to summarize the results of the conversation and experiment, or ask students to write individual summaries about the experiment. Other experiments involving sound and the senses include feeling sound by using a cymbal and feeling the vibrations, tasting sound by eating potato chips, smelling sound as frying bacon or popping popcorn, or hearing sound.

FEELING SOUND VIBRATIONS

Students willl improve their concept of sound by feeling vibrations on a triangle or cymbal.

Procedure

This activity should be included in a unit on the study of the production of sound. Two students come to the front of the class with one student holding a triangle or cymbal and the other standing a few feet away. As the students both close their eyes the teacher should strike the cymbal or triangle. When the student holding the instrument can no longer feel the sound he should raise his hand and when the other student can no longer hear the sound he should raise his hand. Students in the class observing should find that first *they* cannot hear the sound, then the student closest to the instrument cannot hear the sound, and last the person holding the instrument cannot feel the sound. This will prove that because of the vibrations sound can be felt even after it cannot be heard.

Evaluation

Evaluation will be determined through discussion and conclusions of the experiment. Several students should go in front of the class to prove that the results are the same every time. Different instruments may be used and conclusions may be listed on the board as students describe the results of the activity.

CLASSIFICATION OF TIMBRE

Students will improve their concept of timbre by finding items in the room that produce sound and classifying these sounds into various categories.

Procedure

The teacher should give students a few minutes to find an object in the room that can produce a sound. After finding an object each sound should be played, discussed, and categorized as dull, shrill, bright, intense (any descriptions students can use to classify are acceptable). The teacher should introduce the word "timbre" as this discussion and classification takes place.

Evaluation

The teacher must evaluate students by the discussion of classification and the categorizing of the instruments. Further evaluation can be made as the teacher asks students to find other objects with different timbre in certain categories.

PLAY YOUR INSTRUMENT

Students will improve their concept of instruments and timbre by playing different instruments to the tune of "If You're Happy and You Know It."

Procedure

The teacher may choose several students and give each an instrument, such as a tambourine, a woodblock, or a triangle. As the class sings the song "If You're Happy and You Know It" students play their instruments in the proper place

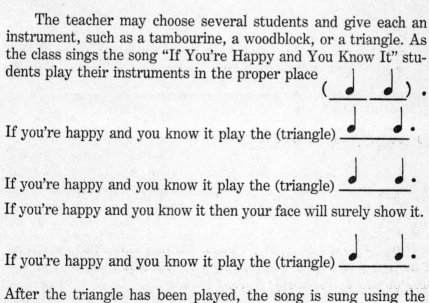

If you're happy and you know it play the (triangle) _____

If you're happy and you know it play the (triangle) _____

If you're happy and you know it then your face will surely show it.

If you're happy and you know it play the (triangle) _____

After the triangle has been played, the song is sung using the woodblock, then the tambourine, then all three instruments together. Different sets of instruments should be used (or even pictures of band instruments could be used) and when the class claps the person in front holds up the card with the proper instrument.

Evaluation

This activity may be evaluated by observing which instruments are played and if they are played in the proper place on the beat. Further evaluation may take place by questioning students about the instruments as the sets of instruments are changed.

TIMBRE OF OBJECTS

Students will improve their concept of timbre by bringing objects from home to produce sound.

Procedure

Students may be asked to bring objects from home, such as tools, kitchen supplies, metal, wood, or glass objects. Each instrument may remain a secret and students can take turns playing them. The rest of the students must try to guess what the instrument is and what material it is made of.

Evaluation

As the teacher refers to each sound as "the timbre of the instrument" this concept will be reinforced. If students perform the activity with no relation to the concept of timbre it will be of little value.

CHARACTER TIMBRE

Students will improve their concept of timbre by selecting appropriate instruments or sounds for various characters.

Procedure

The teacher may begin this activity by playing *Peter and the Wolf* and discussing instruments used for different characters. Students may then select a story with characters as "The Three

Pigs," "The Three Bears," or "The Three Billy Goats Gruff." After the story has been chosen each character should be discussed determining size, kind of voice (high or low), dynamics, how they move (fast or slow). Finally a suitable instrument should be chosen for each character.

Example: "The Three Billy Goats Gruff"
Troll—Big, low, loud, slow—Low notes on piano

Billy Goat 1—Small, high, soft, allegro—Xylophone

Billy Goat 2—Medium, middle, medium soft, moderato— Tambourine

Billy Goat 3—Big, low, loud, adagio—Bass drum

Students may then perform the story and substitute sounds whenever possible.

Evaluation

Evaluation should take place as students discuss and select instruments to represent the different characters. The teacher may offer suggestions, but the students should offer criticism and tell why they think one instrument would be better than another. Students may also be evaluated as they perform the story, possibly for another class.

LABELING INSTRUMENTS

Students will improve their concept of timbre by labeling classroom instruments according to methods of playing, families, and pitch.

Procedure

Instruments should be classified according to Method of Playing (hit, shake, scrape, blow, pluck), Family (strings, woodwind, percussion, brass), and Pitch (high, medium, low). Examples of such classification might be as follows:

Instrument	Method of Playing	Family	Pitch
Woodblock	Hit	Percussion	Medium
Piano	Hit	Percussion, String	High, Medium, Low
Maraca	Shake	Percussion	Medium
Guitar	Pluck	String	High, Medium, Low
Tuba	Blow	Brass	Low
Flute	Blow	Woodwind	High

Evaluation

The teacher may evaluate students by their discussion and classification of instruments. If disagreement occurs about certain instruments the teacher may give her opinion or list both answers in the proper column. This activity may later be used in the form of a written examination as the teacher plays the instruments and students classify them according to Method of Playing, Family and Pitch.

TIMBRE GUESSING GAME

Students will improve their concept of timbre by playing a guessing game.

Procedure

The students should stand in a circle, each holding a different rhythm instrument. In another part of the room (where the class cannot see) one student should stand at a table containing all of the different rhythm instruments held by the other students. The players play four steady beats and then take four beats to pass the instrument to the left, play again, then pass:

Play   2   3   4
Pass   2   3   4
Play   2   3   4
Pass   2   3   4

At some point the teacher says "Stop" and the student at the table plays an instrument. Whoever in the circle has the instrument and can identify the instrument played becomes the leader and the game continues.

Evaluation

Students should be able to identify the instrument played by the leader. If students are not able to do this, the teacher should review timbre and give the students many opportunities to use instruments in class. This activity may be extended to a written test later as the teacher plays the instruments and students identify them.

SOUND STORY

Students will improve their concept of timbre by making a sound story.

Procedure

Students should be divided into several groups and asked to choose a subject for a sound story. Some appropriate titles might include "A Haunted House," "A Rainstorm," "Getting Up in the Morning," "The Barnyard," "The Zoo," "Outside in Spring," or "Fun in the Ocean." After a title has been chosen, students should select all the sounds they can use for their story (either body sounds or instruments may be used) and decide upon a sequence. Once the story is completed (using only sounds) the students may perform the story for the rest of the class. As the class listens they should try to tell what is happening by the sounds that are used.

Evaluation

The sound stories may be considered successful if students are able to guess what is happening. Even if the exact sequence of the story is not guessed, the mood or parts of the story may be discovered. Suggestions may be offered by the teacher or students to improve the stories using different timbres to produce better results.

INSTRUMENTAL ACCOMPANIMENTS

Students will improve their concept of timbre by choosing appropriate instruments to accompany a song.

Procedure

Several songs of various moods, tempo and style should be selected which the students know well. The teacher may then guide students in selecting appropriate instruments for an accompaniment of each song. This activity may also be used with poems of various moods and styles that contain many "sound" words. When making decisions regarding the best combination, the timbre of the instruments should be discussed and different sets of instruments used to produce the final result.

Evaluation

The teacher may evaluate students by their final product, that is, playing the songs and adding their accompaniment. The students should have made a number of conclusions and evaluations themselves while discussing timbre and determining the best choice of instruments. The teacher should be careful not to tell the students which instruments she (he) feels is best, but let them decide by experimentation. There may be differences of opinion in the group so each person should tell why he does (or does not) like the combination of instruments chosen and then vote for a final choice.

DESK SOUNDS

Students will improve their concept of timbre by improvising a composition using sounds from their desks.

Procedure

The teacher should ask each student to perform three sounds from his desk and let the class listen to the timbre of each sound. Students should then be divided into groups of five or six and a conductor selected for each group. The students may have from five to ten minutes to plan a composition led by the conductor using various forms, tempi, dynamics, moods, and textures. Each group may perform their composition for the other groups who will listen and describe the various elements that were used.

Evaluation

Students may be evaluated by their selection of three sounds, their discussion of these sounds and their final composition and performance of these sounds. When evaluating the compositions (along with the students) emphasis should be put on ways to improve the composition or other ways to perform it. Some questions that might be asked are:

1. Did the composition have a good plan?
2. Did the music hold together?
3. What did you like about the composition?
4. How would you change it?
5. How did the conductor perform?

TAPE RECORDER TIMBRE

Students will increase their knowledge of sound by experimenting with the tape recorder.

Procedure

The teacher should demonstrate the following techniques on the tape recorder:

1. Playing the tape backwards
2. Recording at one speed and playing at another
3. Splicing together tapes
4. Recording on top of another tape
5. Speeding up the recorder

After students can handle the recorder and tapes they may be divided into groups assuming there are several recorders. If several recorders are not available, the teacher may select two or three students to take suggestions from the class and make a sound composition using the techniques previously described.

Evaluation

Students may listen to all of the compositions and try to tell how each sound effect was accomplished. When evaluating compostions and students, various techniques and elements should be considered, such as, unity and variety, mood, texture, tempo, or dynamics.

LISTING SOUNDS

Students will improve their concept of timbre by making a list of all the sounds they can think of.

Procedure

Students should make a list of all the sounds that they can think of. This may be done with a time limit in class, as a homework project, or as a game with two teams.

Evaluation

Students may be evaluated by the number of sounds contained on their lists. This list alone will not assure that students have learned the concept of timbre, so many other activities should be used as reinforcement.

SOUNDS AROUND

Students will improve their concept of timbre by closing their eyes and identifying sounds around them.

Procedure

The teacher should ask students to close their eyes and listen for two or three minutes to the sounds around them. After listening, a list may be constructed on the board as students raise their hands and contribute answers. The timbre of these sounds should then be discussed in terms of high, low, dark, bright, click, thud, resonating, or any other descriptive words that can be used.

Evaluation

Evaluation of the students' concept of timbre will be established during the conversation when sounds are described. Further evaluation may be made by a written or oral test.

INSTRUMENTAL FAMILIES

Students will improve their concept of instruments and families of instruments by showing the correct instrument when a certain family is named.

Procedure

After students have studied instruments and families of instruments the teacher may make tags with instrument names. Each student will have one tag and when a family is called by the teacher as "Strings" everyone with a stringed instrument tag comes forward and faces the class. After students are seated again another family is called and the game continues.

Evaluation

The teacher may evaluate by observing which students come forward. Instrument tags should be changed often so that students can work with various families. Further activities and evaluation include making a bulletin board or preparing a scrap book on the instruments and families.

CONSTRUCTING INSTRUMENTS

Students will improve their concept of timbre by making instruments.

Procedure

This project should be given as a homework assignment since it is a time consuming activity and most of the materials will be

found at home. Students may be very creative in their production
of instruments and a contest could be held to determine the best
construction of instruments. Some instruments that might be constructed include:

1. Tambourine: made of coffee can lid and pop bottle caps
2. Maracas: made of gourds
3. Drums: made of small and large cans and rubber heads
4. Stringed instruments: made of bleach bottles, boards,
   and fish lines
5. Bells: made of flower pots and string
6. Harps: made of wooden frame and rubber bands
7. Wood Blocks: made of various sizes of wood
8. Sand Blocks: made of wood and sand paper
9. Whistles: made of wood or bamboo
10. Xylophones: made of metal or wooden bars

Evaluation

The teacher may evaluate students by their workmanship and
originality demonstrated on their finished products. Evaluation of
musical concepts learned will occur through listening and discussion of the instruments. A final means of evaluation might include
an original percussion composition using their instruments or an
instrumental accompaniment to a song used in class.

MATCHING SOUNDS

Students will improve their concept of timbre by matching
sounds.

Procedure

The teacher should prepare several small containers with
matching contents, such as two with rocks, two with salt, two with
paper clips, two with bits of papers, and two with an eraser. Next
the students shake the containers and try to match the pairs by
listening to the timbre of each one. A variation of this activity is to
have one container of each item and students arrange the pitches
from low to high.

Evaluation

The teacher may walk about the room observing or prepare an answer sheet so that students can correct themselves. If only one set of containers is available, students may help evaluate by telling the student in front of the class shaking the containers which is the correct order.

IDENTIFICATION OF INSTRUMENTS

Students may improve their concept of timbre by telling what instruments are used in a recording.

Procedure

Students should have many experiences listening to recordings and identifying the instruments used. This may be done in the form of listing, filling in a work sheet, or discussion as a record is played. Early experiences may include only discussion and, as students advance, listing and worksheets may be used.

Evaluation

The activity of identifying instruments in a recording is a final goal to be achieved when working with the concept of timbre. Students should be able to identify the sound, describe the timbre, and tell why it is appropriate for that particular section of the composition.

WHAT'S THE INSTRUMENT?

Students will improve their concept of timbre by identifying instruments from a tape recorder.

Procedure

The teacher may record various instruments using instruments in the room or asking band and orchestra members to play a short example for recording. The instruments may be recorded, followed by a short pause, and the name of the instrument stated.

In this way students may work alone and immediately know if they had the correct answer.

Evaluation

The students may evaluate themselves as they work alone on this activity. The activity could also be given as a written exam if the names are left off the recording.

Chapter 4

Activities for Teaching Rhythm and Movement

Activities in this section will deal with concepts concerning beat, rhythm, movement and coordination. Methods for presenting note values and rhythmic notation will be included as well as techniques to improve students' coordination through rhythmic exercises and dancing.

NAMES IN RHTYHM

Students will improve their concept of rhythm by clapping names and converting them into rhythm syllables.

Procedure

Each student should clap the rhythm of his name and then convert it to rhythm syllables ("Randy Smith—Ti-ti, ta"). Students may then go to the board and notate the rhythm for the class.

Evaluation

The teacher may observe students to see if they are able to clap the rhythms of their names, convert them to rhythm syllables and notate them properly. This activity should begin in first grade and continue throughout elementary school by the use of worksheets and various words or phrases.

NAME NOTATION

Students will improve their concept of rhythm by notating students' names from a work sheet.

Procedure

After students have had several experiences clapping names and converting them to rhythm syllables the teacher may hand out a work sheet with everyone's name in the class. The students should complete the sheet and return it to the teacher for evaluation.

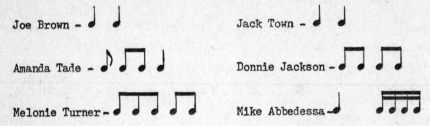

Evaluation

The teacher may notate rhythms on the board and let the students check their own papers or collect the papers for evaluation. Some names may be notated more than one way, so all possibilities should be considered correct.

RHYTHM GAME

Students will improve their rhythm skills by playing a game called "Rhythm."

Procedure

The teacher may introduce the mechanics of this game by having students slap their legs two times, clap two times, and snap two times (first with one hand, then with the other). Students must be able to repeat this sequence without losing the beat before the game can be continued.

Slap	Slap	Clap	Clap	Snap	Snap
				(right)	(left)

As everyone is performing the sequence together, the teacher says her name on the first snap and a student's name on the second snap. It is then that student's turn and when the snaps occur again he must say his name on the first snap and another student's on the second snap.

Slap	Slap	Clap	Clap	Snap		Snap
♩	♩	♩	♩	♩		♩

Teacher	"	"	"	"	"Mrs. Smith"	"Bobby"
Bobby	"	"	"	"	"Bobby"	"Sue"
Sue	"	"	"	"	"Sue"	"Melissa"
Melissa	"	"	"	"	"Melissa"	"John"

When a person loses the beat or says a name in the wrong rhythm he must be seated and the teacher begins the game again until only the champion remains.

Evaluation

At first students will be slow and many will drop out quickly. After the game has been played several times, students will be able to pick up the tempo and improve their coordination. The teacher may observe students who have difficulty and provide extra coordination exercises when needed. This is also an excellent means of occupying the class when the teacher must leave the room unexpectedly. A leader can be chosen to start the game, and they will be involved in a constructive activity until the teacher can return.

PHRASE NOTATION

Students will improve their ability to work with rhythms by notating a phrase or poem.

Procedure

After students have had experience notating names and various words, the teacher may introduce the notation of phrases or poems. The phrase should be repeated and clapped several times, bringing attention to the accents. Students may then notate the rhythm of the words at the board, orally from their seats, or on individual papers.

Phrases: Halloween Night

                Jingle all the Way

                Easter eggs are Everywhere

Poem: Jack be nimble, Jack be quick

                Jack jumped over the candle stick

Evaluation

After students have notated rhythms orally and at the board the teacher may wish to give a written examination for evaluation. There may be several possibilities for the notation of these phrases or sentences so variations may be discussed by the students and teacher. An extension of this activity includes creating a poem and notating its rhythm for an original composition.

MOVING TO MUSIC

Students will improve their rhythm skills and coordination by moving to drum patterns.

Procedure

One student is chosen to be the leader and play various rhythms on the drum. As these rhythms are played the remainder of the class should move to the music:

The rhythm should be played as students move, a pause while students become "still like statues," and a new rhythm played as the students move again. This is continued until all the rhythms have been attempted several times and a new leader is chosen.

Evaluation

The teacher may evaluate students by observing which students are able to detect the change in the drum pattern and move accordingly. If a student is having difficulty, the teacher may move close to him and perform the correct movement as the drum is played, or have students move in pairs—one with good coordination and one who needs help.

RHYTHM IDENTIFICATION

Students will improve their concept of rhythm by playing and identifying certain rhythm patterns.

Procedure

The teacher should have four rhythm patterns notated on the board:

A student may be asked to play a certain pattern, or he may choose one and play it, having the class guess which one he played. In the upper grades, more difficult patterns using triplets, sixteenth notes, and syncopated patterns may be used.

Evaluation

The teacher should observe to discover if students are able to play and identify the correct patterns. This may also be used as a written examination with the teacher playing the pattern and students listing the correct number. If students are unable to perform this activity, more experiences should be provided for them to use and notate rhythms in songs and games.

DUPLE AND TRIPLE METER

Students will develop an awareness of duple and triple meter by clapping and playing instruments with accents and listening to records in duple and triple meter.

Procedure

The teacher should clap or play an instrument using steady beats with no accents. When students are asked if the beat was in twos or threes there may be various answers until the teacher says, "We couldn't tell if it went in twos or threes—now listen." A rhythm in duple meter may be clapped and identified, then one in triple meter demonstrated. Students should discuss this demonstration and find that an accent always occurs on the first beat, so meter may be identified in sets of twos or threes. Students may experiment with this concept by using body sounds or rhythm instruments in sets of twos (clap-snap, patting knees-clap, tambourine-triangle) or threes (tap-whistle-whistle, jump-snap-snap, woodblock-sticks-sticks). Finally, students may listen to records and identify the meter in sets of twos or threes.

Evaluation

The means of evaluation is the final activity listed in the above procedure. If students are able to hear and identify duple and triple meter on records, they have gained the concept. Later the teacher may move to changing meter and combinations of duple and triple meter in fives or sevens.

BEAT AND MELODIC RHYTHM

Students will improve their concept of beat and melodic rhythm by tapping the beat with their feet and clapping the melodic rhythm.

Procedure

Students should have had previous experience clapping the beat and the melodic rhythm of songs.

1. The teacher may ask students to clap the beat of a song.
2. The teacher may ask students to clap the melodic rhythm of a song.
3. The teacher may clap the beat or melodic rhythm of songs and ask students to identify which were clapped.
4. The teacher may choose a student to clap the beat or melodic rhythm and let the class identify which was clapped. The student who gives the correct answer becomes the leader.

After students are familiar with both concepts (beat and melodic rhythm), the teacher may ask them to put the beat in their feet and clap the melodic rhythm with their hands. This may be varied by clapping the beat and tapping the melodic rhythm with the feet.

Evaluation

The teacher may observe to see which students are coordinated and can perform two different tasks at one time. This activity should not be attempted until students understand the difference in beat and melodic rhythm and can clap (or tap) one at a time.

ACTION SONGS

Students will improve their rhythm skills by performing various actions to phrases or key words in a song.

Procedure

The teacher may use any song that students have been singing which has been memorized. As the song is divided into sections or phrases, various actions should be selected for each key word or phrase. Students may be very creative in their selection of actions and should be encouraged to invent new motions for different songs.

"John Brown Had a Little Indian"—Have ten students and each one pops up or down when their number is sung.
"Twinkle Twinkle Little Star"—Phrase 1—Turn in a circle
                                            Phrase 2—Clap the beat
                                            Phrase 3—Turn in a circle
"Paw Paw Patch"—Verse 1—Clap hands together with part-
                                            ner
                    Verse 2—March
                    Verse 3—Pretend to pick up paw paws

Evaluation

Rhythm skills may be the result of good coordination in body movements used with songs and handling musical instruments. The teacher may evaluate students by observing their movements and determining which students need help. The students' coordination is important in all school subjects, such as physical education (coordination in playing games), reading (eye movement across the page), or writing (holding a pencil and smooth movements). Music is an excellent opportunity for students to improve body coordination through rhythm and movement.

RHYTHM DETECTIVES

Students will improve their concept of melodic rhythm by identifying songs by their rhythms.

Procedure

The teacher should make a list of songs that are known by all students, such as:

1. "Twinkle Twinkle Little Star"   6. "Happy Birthday"
2. "Are You Sleeping?"   7. "Jingle Bells"
3. "Silent Night"   8. "Bingo"
4. "America"   9. "Tinga Layo"
5. "This Old Man"   10. "Oh Susanna"

The leader must choose a song and clap the melodic rhythm. The student who can name the song then becomes the leader and the game continues.

Evaluation

This is an excellent means of ear training as well as a reinforcement for rhythm. If students have trouble identifying the songs, some may be dropped from the list. At times the leader may not clap the correct rhythm so the teacher can ask him to repeat the example or choose another song.

RHYTHM DIAGRAMS

Students will improve their concept of rhythm by translating the rhythm of music into designs on paper.

Procedure

The teacher may use this activity after students have worked with the concept of rhythm in music, painting, lines, nature, and sounds. As a record is played students should translate the rhythm of the music into designs on paper with crayons or paint. These papers may be discussed and displayed about the room or used as a bulletin board arrangement.

Evaluation

The teacher may evaluate students by their discussion and explanation of their picture. Although no certain pattern is "right" or "wrong," evaluation may be determined by individual interpretations. Each student should explain how his picture relates to the rhythm of the recording.

CONDUCTING SONGS

Students will improve their concept of beat by identifying the meter and conducting songs.

Procedure

The teacher should select several songs in various meters that the students know by memory. As a song is played and sung the students should determine whether the beat goes in twos, threes, fours, or sixes. Students then use the correct conducting pattern as they repeat the song with everyone singing and conducting.

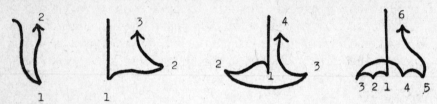

The teacher may find it necessary to list the various conducting patterns on the board and lead the students as they practice each pattern before conducting with songs.

Evaluation

The teacher may evaluate students as the conducting patterns are performed. Items that should be noted include using the correct pattern, conducting in the correct direction, using smooth movements, and staying with the beat. Many songs and recordings in different meters should be used so that students have many experiences using conducting patterns.

MEMORY RHYTHM NOTATION

Students will improve their concept of rhythmic notation by clapping a song from memory and notating the rhythm.

Procedure

Simple songs that the students know well should be used for this activity. Students clap a phrase of the song by memory, notate it, and continue to the next phrase until the complete song has been notated. This notation should be written on the board so that all the students can see and correct any mistakes.

Evaluation

The teacher should use a song contained in the students' books, so that after the song has been notated on the board the students may open their books to check their notation. Mistakes should be corrected and the song may be sung with an appropriate accompaniment.

RHYTHM BOUNCING BALL

Students will improve their concept of beat by passing objects and bouncing a ball on the beat.

Procedure

Recordings or songs should be used that have a strong, steady beat and an even tempo. As students listen or sing they should pass an object to the beat or bounce a ball on the beat. If a bouncing ball is used students may bounce to the person standing either next to them or across the circle. Everyone must be alert because they never know when they will receive the ball. If the beat is lost students must feel the beat and begin the ball (or object) again.

Evaluation

Students may not be able to keep the beat by passing objects or bouncing a ball for a very long period at first. Improvement may be determined by the length of time the students can continue without losing the beat. After students can perform the activity with ease, it may be used as a contest by having students drop out when they lose the beat until only the champion remains.

THINKING THE BEAT

Students will improve their concept of beat and tempo by thinking the beat and coming in together.

Procedure

Any song that the students know well may be used for this activity. After the song is sung several times the teacher should select one phrase where students will not sing but think the melody. This phrase must be somewhere in the middle of the song to see if students can come in together after "putting the words on the inside of themselves."

"Twinkle Twinkle Little Star"

Sing: Twinkle twinkle little star
        How I wonder what you are

Think: Up above the world so high
        Like a diamond in the sky

Sing: Twinkle twinkle little star
        How I wonder what you are

After thinking the melody students should come in together on the last phrase.

Evaluation

If students do not come in together on the last phrase, the teacher may have them clap as they think, whisper the words, or whistle on the silent phrase. This is an excellent illustration to show students that music takes a great deal of concentration and must be exact to stay together.

POLYRHYTHMS

Students will improve their understanding of polyrhythms by chanting words in different meters simultaneously.

Procedure

Students should select words with different numbers of syllables and ones which have accents that fall in different places. If it is close to a holiday, appropriate words may be used to correspond with the season:

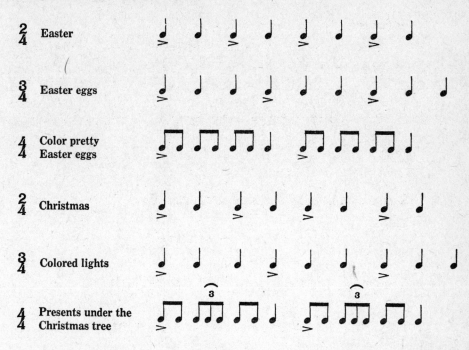

Each word or phrase should be clapped separately until the rhythm, beats, and accents are performed correctly. The class may then be divided into three groups, and each group claps its phrase while the other two groups clap different phrases. The result is polyrhythms.

Evaluation

The teacher should first evaluate students as they clap the phrases separately. Before attempting all three phrases together, the class could be divided into two groups and different combinations of two phrases clapped together. Finally, the teacher should decide when the class is ready to try all three rhythms simultaneously.

SYNCOPATION DETECTIVE

Students will improve their concept of syncopation by finding examples of syncopated rhythms in their song book.

Procedure

After students have had some experience with syncopated rhythms (singing songs, listening to recordings, and discussing the term and meaning) the teacher may list ways on the chalkboard that syncopation can be accomplished:

1. By accenting a normally weak beat:

2. By having a rest on a strong beat:

3. By holding a weak beat over a strong beat:

4. By tying a weak portion of a beat to a stronger one:

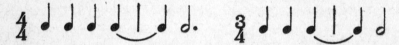

After students have discussed each example, the teacher should ask them to look through their song books to find examples of syncopation. As a page is called, everyone may turn to that page and discuss how the syncopation has been accomplished.

Evaluation

The teacher may evaluate students as they find examples and discuss ways in which the composer accomplished syncopation. Examples may be discussed, clapped, played on rhythm instruments, and finally the song may be sung. This activity forces students to apply their knowledge of syncopation and gives the teacher an accurate means of evaluation.

SYNCOPATED AND
UNSYNCOPATED RHYTHMS

Students will improve their understanding of syncopation by identifying examples as unsyncopated or syncopated rhythms.

Procedure

The teacher may clap a series of rhythms, pausing after each rhythm for students to identify it as unsyncopated or syncopated. Various meters should be used so that the students become familar with syncopated patterns in various situations. Examples that the teacher might clap include the following:

Unsyncopated   Syncopated

Evaluation

Instead of having the class call out the answers together, the teacher may have them raise their hands for a more accurate evaluation. The most effective means of evaluation would be a written test where the teacher claps the rhythm and the students write the answers. The papers could be corrected by the students and collected by the teacher to see which students need additional help.

"POP" MUSIC AND BEAT

Students will improve their rhythmic skills by clapping in various ways to a "pop" recording.

Procedure

This is an excellent opportunity for the teacher to use "pop" records that students bring to school. The teacher can communicate with students by showing acceptance of the music they appreciate, yet, a worthwhile rhythmic activity is accomplished. As the record is played the teacher should call out different counts to be clapped. After clapping a short time, new numbers may be called and clapped. (Quotation marks represent the teacher's voice).

"1 and 3—1, 2, ready, go"—clap on beats 1 and 3—"Stop"
"2 and 4—1, 2, ready, go"—clap on beats 2 and 4—"Stop"
"1 and 4—1, 2, ready, go"—clap on beats 1 and 4—"Stop"

Another variation of counting and clapping to "pop" music includes clapping in series of eights leaving off one count each time until there is silence and building back up to eight again. (Dashes indicate rests).

1	2	3	4	5	6	7	8
1	2	3	4	5	6	7	—
1	2	3	4	5	6	—	—
1	2	3	4	5	—	—	—
1	2	3	4	—	—	—	—

1	2	3	—	—	—	—	—
1	2	—	—	—	—	—	—
1	—	—	—	—	—	—	—
—	—	—	—	—	—	—	—
1	—	—	—	—	—	—	—
1	2	—	—	—	—	—	—
1	2	3	—	—	—	—	—
1	2	3	4	—	—	—	—
1	2	3	4	5	—	—	—
1	2	3	4	5	6	—	—
1	2	3	4	5	6	7	—
1	2	3	4	5	6	7	8

A third variation involves dividing the class into groups and drawing a chart on the chalkboard to indicate on which counts each group claps (clap on the dark areas).

Evaluation

Students may be evaluated by their ability to clap on the correct beats, which will take both coordination and concentration. Students must first be able to clap the beat before divisions of counts presented in this activity should be attempted. The teacher is always in the process of evaluation, determining when students are ready to advance one step further, or when they need to go back and review concepts. A great deal of this evaluation is accomplished through observation as students perform various activities.

CREATING DANCES

Students will improve their rhythmic skills by moving to music and creating line dances.

Procedure

This is an excellent opportunity to allow students to use "pop" records and at the same time accomplish good coordination and exercise in rhythmic skills. The class should begin with simple actions to "pop" records and proceed to longer and more difficult combination of actions. As a record is played in duple meter, the following activity should be performed:

1	2	3	4	1	2	3	4
Step	Clap	Step	Clap	Step	Clap	Step	Clap
Right		Left		Right		Left	

At first this exercise may be done standing in place and then bending the knees on every clap. Finally, students should try to walk around the room to the music still using the "step clap" sequence.

	1	2	3	4	1	2	3	4
March	Left	Right	Left	Right	Left	Right	Left	Right
Snap fingers—	Snap	Snap	Snap	Snap	Snap	Snap	Snap	Snap

(1 and 2 on the right)
(3 and 4 on the left)

As students march in place and snap their fingers they should be encouraged to bounce, sway, or swing as long as the steps and snaps are continued in the proper rhythm. Later they may move about the room using this step to "pop" records and adjusting their tempo to that of the record.

1	2	3	4	1	2	3	4
Bump	Out	Bump	Out	Bump	Out	Bump	Out
1	2	3	4	1	2	3	4
Bump	Out	Bump	Out	Bump	Out	Bump	Out

Students should work in partners for this activity bumping hips together on counts one and three and swinging out on counts two and four (or bumping on counts one and two and swinging out on three and four).

Students may try various other combinations of movements to their "pop" records using sets of four counts:

1	2	3	4	1	2	3	4
Step	Kick	Step	Kick	Step	Kick	Step	Kick

	1	2	3	4
Forward:	Step	Step	Step	Kick
Backward:	Step	Step	Step	Kick
To the Right:	Step	Slide	Step	Slide
To the Left:	Step	Slide	Step	Slide

Many experiments and different combinations may be used until a line is created where students stand in a line (or two lines), face each other, and perform a sequence of steps to the music:

All students face North in one line

	1	2	3	4
Move to the right:	Step	Slide	Step	Slide
	Right	Left	Right	Left
Move to the Left:	Step	Slide	Step	Slide
	Left	Right	Left	Right
Move Backwards:	Step	Slide	Step	Slide
	Right	Left	Right	Left
Stand in Place:	Tap	Clap	Tap	Turn (West)
	Left Toe		Left Toe	

Face West and repeat sequence turning to the South.
Face South and repeat sequence turning to the East.
Face East and repeat sequence turning to the North.
Continue to the end of the record.

Evaluation

Students must be evaluated at each stage, accomplishing easy
steps before advancing to more difficult movements until a line
dance is created and performed without mistakes. If students have
difficulty with certain movements, the teacher should offer activities which will reinforce that movement. Some students will
master the skills quickly, but a few students may never be able to
perform an entire line dance without mistakes. Encouragement
and repetition should give the students confidence and greater skill
with fewer mistakes.

RHYTHM CHARTS

Students will improve their concept of rhythm and notation by
filling in charts.

Procedure

The teacher may guide students in filling out the following
chart and later use it as a written test for evaluation:

Movement	Line Notation	Words	Music Notation
Walk, Hop, Clap	— — — —	ta ta ta ta	♩ ♩ ♩ ♩
Tap, Run, Clap	-- -- -- --	ti-ti-ti-ti	♫ ♫ ♫ ♫
Skip Gallop	——–—	ta-ti-ta-ti	♩ ♪ ♩ ♪
Sway, Slide, Skate, Swing	————	ta-a-a	♩.
Step, Bend, Jump	—— ——	ta-a ta-a	♩ ♩

Evaluation

This chart will help students to be aware of different methods of symbolizing rhythms. It will be necessary to work with the students, using various movements and forms of notation before they will be able to fill in the chart correctly. The chart may be the final activity used as a means of evaluation of rhythmic concepts. If students do poorly on the chart, review is needed. If they do well, the teacher may move on to new and more difficult concepts.

ACCENTS

Students will improve their concept of accents and meter by reading line notation and identifying the meter that is used.

Procedure

The teacher should have the following chart listed on the board:

The teacher may let students experiment, clapping all the examples and bringing attention to the dark accented lines. The term "accent" should be discussed, relating sets of twos, threes, fours, fives, sixes, or sevens. Each example should be clapped and discussed. At this point the teacher may present the standard notation:

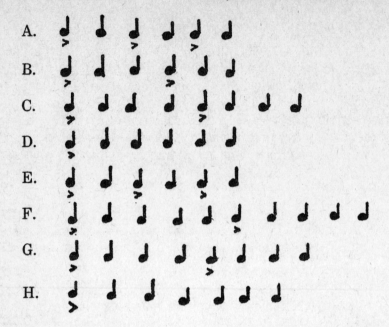

A leader should be chosen to clap one of the examples as the class guesses which one was clapped. The student who answers correctly becomes the leader and the game continues.

Evaluation

The teacher may evaluate the effectiveness of this lesson by the final activity, following each example of notation where students must clap one of the examples and the class must identify which example was clapped.

NOTE VALUE CHARTS

Students will improve their concept of note values by observing or filling in charts.

Procedure

Many charts can be made that represent note values. These charts may be observed, discussed, copied, or used as a test.

NOTE VALUES

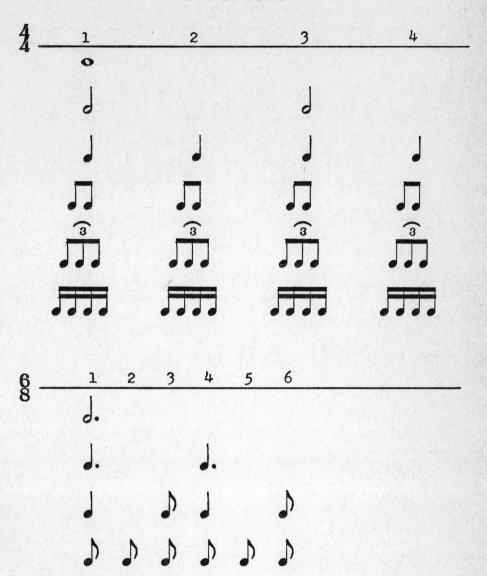

Students should apply this chart by using the information to fill in measures with the correct number of counts or to compose songs.

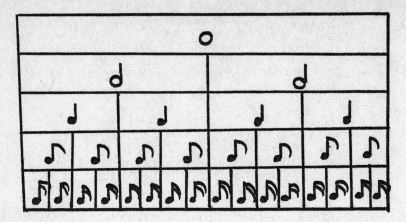

This chart should be handed to students omitting the note values. Students fill in the notes beginning at the top with a whole note and working down to the sixteenth notes for reinforcement of note values.

By using this chart students will achieve a better understanding of the relationship of note values. The teacher may ask questions that can be answered from the chart after the blank chart has been completed by the students.

How many sixteenth notes does it take to equal four eighth notes?
How many quarter notes does it take to equal two half notes?
How many quarter notes does it take to equal one whole note?
How many quarter rests does it take to equal one whole rest?
Question with any combination of notes that can be answered by referring to the chart.

Red—Sixteenth Notes or Rests
Yellow—Eighth Notes or Rests
Blue—Quarter Notes or Rests
Green—Half Notes or Rests
Orange—Whole Notes or Rests

As students color the balls they must recognize the note in order to give it the proper color. This idea may be used as a seasonal activity using Easter eggs, turkey with tail feathers, valentine hearts or witches and monsters.

Evaluation

Evaluation will depend on the method used to present each chart. If charts are observed and discussed, the teacher should listen and question students, asking how many of one type of notes equals another kind of note. After discussion and copying charts, the students may be asked to fill in a chart as a written test. The teacher may correct the papers and determine if more experience of this kind is necessary.

RHYTHM CARDS

Students will improve their concept of rhythm by arranging rhythm cards and clapping the different combinations.

Procedure

The teacher should prepare colored cards with note values in proportion to their size.

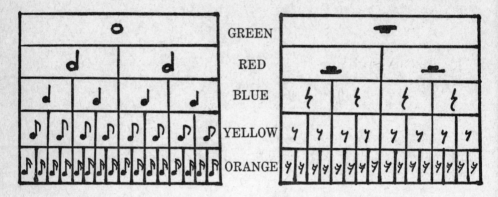

Each card should be separate so that the students can arrange them in various combinations.

Cards may be stacked in separate piles as the leader comes to the front of the room to arrange a four count example. The class claps the example and a new leader is chosen to arrange another four count example. Lower grades may work only with whole, quarter, and half notes and rests and upper grades may advance to eighth and sixteenth notes and rests after succeeding with many combinations of lower note values.[5]

Evaluation

The teacher may evaluate the leader as he arranges a four count example. This may be varied, using different time signatures, such as 2/4, 3/2, 6/8 or any other time signature. The class may help the leader if a mistake has been made and therefore aid in

[5]Eugene L. Beenk, *Music Teachers Resource Manual*. (Iowa, Music Educator Aids, 1974) Contributed by Mrs. Mary Rother.

the evaluation. If the class cannot clap the example correctly, the teacher may ask an individual student to demonstrate the correct way, allow the class to listen and try again.

MATHEMATICAL RHYTHM

Students will improve their concept of rhythm and note values by working mathematical problems involving rhythms and note values.

Procedure

The teacher may prepare work sheets using the examples given below. Only a few examples are given for each type of problem, but complete pages could be made of any one of these.

RHYTHM CIRCLES

Circle all the rhythms that equal 6.

$\frac{4}{4}$ ♩♩ ⁂ ♩♩   ♩♩ ⁂ ♩   ♩. ♩.   ♩ ⁂ o

Circle all the rhythms that equal 9.

$\frac{3}{2}$ ♩ ♩ o o o ♩   ♩♩♩ o o   ♩o♩o♩o   o⊸ o⊸

Circle all the rhythms that equal 7.

$\frac{6}{8}$ ♪♪♪♩   ♩♩   ♩♪ ⁊ ♪ ⁊   ♩. ♩

Circle all the rhythms that equal 10.

$\frac{3}{4}$ o o ♩   ⁂⁂⁂ ♫♩o♩   ♩♩♩♩♩   ⁊♩o♩

EQUAL VALUES

Draw in the correct amount of notes. The first one is completed for you.

1. ○ ○   =   ♩♩♩♩♩♩♩♩ (Quarter notes)

2. 𝄿♩𝄿○   =   (♩♩♩♩) (Half notes)

3. ♩𝄾𝄿   =   _____ (Eighth notes)

4. ♩♩𝄿   =   _____ (Eighth rests)

5. ○♩♩   =   _____ (Whole notes)

6. ♩♩𝄾𝄿𝄿   =   _____ (Quarter notes)

7. ○♫♫♩   =   _____ (Dotted half notes)

8. ♩♩   =   _____ (Sixteenth notes)

9. ♩𝄿   =   _____ (Eighth rests)

10. ♩♩○   =   _____ (Quarter rests)

NOTE VALUES

○ = (4) Quarter notes   ♪ = (1) Sixteenth notes

♩ = (4) Eighth notes   𝄾 = (4) Sixteenth notes

♩ = (2) Eighth notes   ○ = (16) Sixteenth notes

CHANGING TIME SIGNATURES

$\frac{4}{4}$ ♩ ♩ ♩ ♩♩ 𝄽 = 5
$\qquad$ 1 2 1 1

$\frac{3}{2}$ ♩ ♩ ♩ ♩♩ 𝄽 = 2½
$\qquad$ ½ ½ 1 ½ ½

$\frac{6}{8}$ ♩ ♩ ♩ ♩♩ 𝄽 = 10
$\qquad$ 2 4 2 2

$\frac{4}{4}$ 𝅝 ♩ ♩ ♩

$\frac{3}{2}$ 𝅝 ♩ ♩ ♩

$\frac{6}{8}$ 𝅝 ♩ ♩ ♩

$\frac{4}{4}$ 𝅝 ♩♩ 𝄾 𝄽

$\frac{3}{2}$ 𝅝 ♩♩ 𝄾 𝄽

$\frac{6}{8}$ 𝅝 ♩♩ 𝄾 𝄽

$\frac{4}{4}$ ♩ ♩ ♩ ♩

$\frac{3}{2}$ ♩ ♩ ♩ ♩

$\frac{6}{8}$ ♩ ♩ ♩ ♩

NOTE ADDITION

1. $\frac{3}{2}$ ♪
$\qquad$ + 𝅝/4

2. $\frac{4}{8}$ ♩ + 𝄾 + ♩ + 𝅝 = <u>(16)</u>

3. $\frac{4}{4}$ ♪
$\qquad$ + 𝅝/3

4. $\frac{4}{2}$ 𝄾 + ♩ + 𝅝 + ♩ =

5. $\frac{4}{4}$ ♪
$\qquad$ 𝅗𝅥
$\qquad$ + ♩

6. $\frac{3}{8}$ ♪ + 𝄾 + ♩. + ♩ =

Evaluation

These problems and equations should be worked out by the students and checked by the teacher to see if more help is needed. Such work sheets should aid in the development of the students' concepts of rhythm and note values. These concepts should be applied to songs as they are sung or played in class.

CLAPPING RHYTHM PATTERNS

Students will improve their concept of rhythm patterns by clapping various patterns.

Procedure

The teacher should prepare a set of cards containing rhythm patterns, such as the following:

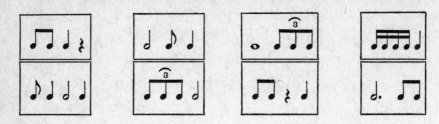

The class should stand by their chairs or in a line at the front of the classroom. The first student should clap the rhythm as the teacher shows a card. If he is not able to clap the pattern he must sit down, or if he can clap it the teacher moves to the next student. The student standing the longest is the winner of the game.

Evaluation

The teacher may evaluate students by their ability to clap the various rhythmic patterns. These patterns should begin on a basic level and advance to more complicated rhythms. The teacher may have the students clap all of the rhythmic patterns together before beginning the game. When students are very familiar with the patterns, it may be impossible to work until only one student remains. In this case, a time limit may be set and everyone remaining at the end is a winner.

RHYTHM GAMEBOARD AND CARDS

Students will improve their understanding of note values by playing a game.

Procedure

Items needed for this game include playing pieces, playing board, and cards.

MAKE FIFTY CARDS

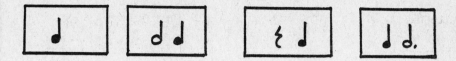

GAME BOARD

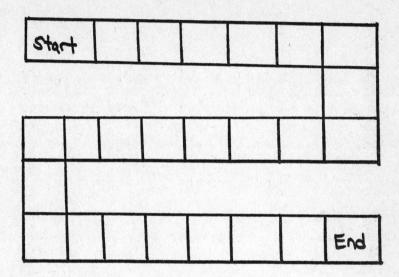

The cards should have rhythm patterns which the student must add to see how many spaces he may move. The class should be divided into two teams. As the first player steps forward he turns up a card and moves his piece appropriately. If the player cannot add the notes correctly the other team may call the mistake, and he loses his turn. The team that is first to reach the "end" of the playing board is the winner.

Evaluation

Students may be evaluated by their ability to add note values. The teacher may use work sheets for reinforcement if additional help is needed.

RHYTHM BEAT

Students will improve their skill and understanding of rhythm by playing the game Rhythm Beat.

Procedure

The class must be divided into teams, A and B. A column of rhythms should be put on the board for each team as follows:

The list should include enough so everyone may try a rhythm, and rhythms should also be equal in difficulty for each team. The first person on team A tries to clap the first rhythm in the A column. If he succeeds he gets a point. If he does not succeed the team does not get the point. Then the first person on Team B gets to try the first rhythm in the B column. When a rhythm is clapped incorrectly, the team does not get the point and the next person on the team must clap the missed rhythm when it is that team's turn again. The team that finishes clapping its column first wins the game.

Evaluation

The teacher must watch to see which students have difficulty clapping the rhythms. The teacher may wish to write the names of these students down and later give them additional help. Flash card drill with examples of rhythms would also be very helpful for these students.

RHYTHM BASEBALL

Students will improve their concept of rhythm by playing Rhythm Baseball.

Procedure

The teacher should prepare a chart with ten or more common rhythm patterns and designate places in the room as bases. The "pitcher" has a rhythm instrument and selects a rhythm pattern from the chart to play on it. The "batter" must look at the chart and guess which pattern was played. If he is correct, he goes to first base and a new batter on that team comes forward. If the pitcher plays an incorrect pattern the batter may walk. After three outs the teams switch.[6]

Evaluation

This is a game with a built-in motivation (baseball). Students may be evaluated by their ability to clap and indentify the rhythms. This may be a time-consuming activity, so a time limit could be set or the game continued over several days.

RHYTHM DICE

Students will improve their recognition of notes and rhythms by playing a game with dice.

---

[6]Eugene L. Beenk, *Music Teacher Resource Manual.* (Iowa, Music Educator Aids, 1974) Contributed by Mrs. Phyllis J. Nelson.

Procedure

Players should have pencils, paper with a common rhythm pattern (♩ 𝄾 ♩ 𝄾 ♪ ♩ 𝅝 ♫ 𝄾), and one die.
Each person takes a turn throwing the die. If the die lands on the first note of the rhythm pattern the student may copy the first note under the original note on the paper. If the die does not land on the first note, the player does not copy any rhythm on his paper and the die goes to the next person. When the die has landed on the first note and the player has copied it on his paper, he may try for the second note on the paper when it is his turn again. The first person to finish copying the rhythm pattern under the original rhythm is the winner.

Evaluation

This is a game that students may play without close supervision from the teacher. The evaluation may take place as the teacher moves about the room observing students, or as the players continue the game and evaluate their own progress.

RHYTHM RELAY

Students will improve their use of note rhythms by playing a Rhythm Relay game.

Procedure

The class should be divided into four teams with five players on each team. Four problems with five measures each should be listed on the chalkboard.

The first person of each team forms a line in front of the room before a problem on the board. When given the signal they add the proper note and give the chalk to the next person who fills in the second measure. The first team to complete the five measures is the winner. Problems may be traded so that students gain experience working with different note values in various time signatures.

Evaluation

The teacher may evaluate students at the board as they fill in the measures. If one team finishes, "time" is called and the teacher checks the example. If it is wrong, the "begin" signal is given and the game continues until one team has completed the example correctly.

Chapter 5

Activities for Developing Musical Creativity

Activities in this section will deal with students' expression of creative ability. Students will employ their creative ideas to dramatize stories and songs, create endings to songs, compose sound stories and complete compositions, and to express themselves through movement and dances.

SPACE MUSIC

Students will improve their ability in creative movement by pretending to be space creatures as they move to the music.

Procedure

The teacher should set the mood of this activity by asking students to close their eyes and imagine that they are a creature in outer space. Ask them to think about where they are in outer space, what their arms, legs, head, etc. look like and how would they move, (big steps, little steps, jerky, smoothly). The students should then be instructed to pretend to be this outer space creature and move to the recording that is played. Every person should have an individual and unique interpretation of the music. This type of activity will free the students' creative ability, and later more complex dances with formal steps can be created.

Evaluation

Activities of this type should be started at an early age and continued into the upper grades. Students in the upper grades may be reluctant to do this type of creative activity at the onset. The teacher should strive to be understanding and offer encouragement to shy students on all grade levels. If the students are participating, the shy student will usually join the others. Additional creative activities include playing tone clusters on the piano as the students move like tigers or elephants, playing light airy music as students move as fairies or birds, or playing various types of music as students move as a character or animal and the remainder of the class tries to guess what it is.

SINGING PUPPETS

Students will further their creative ability by using puppets and singing a conversation.

Procedure

Items needed for this activity include several hand puppets and a stage made from a piano bench, chairs, desk, or a box. The class may decide on the setting and the plot of a story and several students should be chosen to use the puppets. These puppets may be bought, made from paper sacks or socks, brought from home, or made in the art or music classes. The performing students will get behind the stage and sing a conversation using the puppets. Students should be able to improvise the conversation as they go along, using the setting and plot suggested by the class as a guide. This activity is also an excellent introduction to opera.

Evaluation

This is not an activity that the teacher will want to grade or evaluate other than to observe. The children should be able to respond freely without hesitation and the atmosphere should be friendly and free from criticism.

SINGING A STORY

Students will strengthen their creative ability by creating one sentence of a story and singing it or playing it on the bells.

Procedure

After the students and teacher have selected a topic or title for a story, several students should be chosen (any number will do, depending on how long the song will be). The first student should create a sentence pertaining to the topic of the story and sing or play it on the bells. The second person then adds a phrase to the song, singing and playing it on the bellls. The other persons then follow until all the students have played and the composition is finished. Finally, the students should perform the entire composition beginning with the first person and continuing until everyone has played and the song is completed. The key of C (or a pentatonic scale) may be used when creating and playing the song.

Evaluation

The teacher must evaluate students' progress as the story is created and performed. Suggestions for improvement may be offered as students evaluate themselves by deciding if the music fits the words and whether the entire song sounded as if it belonged together. Students may just sing the composition if they find it too difficult to create a melody on the bells and play and sing both.

COMPOSING ENDINGS TO SONGS

Students will improve their creative ability by composing several endings to songs.

Procedure

Students should take turns composing different endings to a song, using a song that is familiar to them. Instruments that should be available include bells, marimba, xylophone, piano, or any melodic instrument that can be used successfully. The students may use the words as they are written and change the melody or change both the words and the melody. At first the students may prefer to sing the ending rather than to use the instrument. Later the students may wish to advance to the use of both the instrument and words.

Evaluation

Students may choose the ending that they like best. The teacher may evaluate the students by watching to see if they are able to write more than one ending and by listening to the students evaluate their own work.

COMPOSITION FROM A DESIGN

Students will further their creative ability by creating a composition from a design on the board.

Procedure

Although there are many ways to create this type of composition, there must be a design to begin with. The teacher should draw the design on the board (or poster paper) so that it may be seen by all of the students, such as the one that follows:

Students may interpret the design by the use of mouth sounds, body sounds, or instruments. The class may work together to create the composition, or committees may be formed to develop the different compositions that could be made from one design. After the composition has been created from the design, a final performance should be given by the class.

Evaluation

Part of this evaluation should be made as the composition is being created and the other part after the final performance. Students who offer suggestions should be recognized and others should be encouraged to do so. The teacher may watch for leaders but should also prevent any one individual from monopolizing the session. The teacher and students may evaluate the final product together noting whether the music corresponds with the design from beginning to end.

CREATING PENTATONIC SONGS

Students will improve their creative skills and concept of oriental music by creating a pentatonic song.

Procedure

The black keys on the piano or melody bells may be used for this activity. Four students should line up in front of the melody bells or piano, one person to compose each of the four phrases of the song. After experimenting, the first person plays a phrase for the class. The second, third, and forth students create a phrase in that order. Finally, the students line up and play their phrase (one, two, three, and four) until the composition has been completed.

Evaluation

Students may evaluate each other as the composition is completed and played. Some questions and areas for discussion include:

1. Were the phrases too long, too short, or about of equal length?
2. Did the students perform their phrases correctly?
3. Was there any hesitation between phrases or did the music flow smoothly?
4. Did the phrases sound as if they belonged together?
5. Is there any part of the composition that could be improved?

The teacher may evaluate students during this discussion and ask any other questions that could lead to a better understanding of the concept and skills to be learned.

CREATING A MAJOR COMPOSITION

Students will improve their creative ability and concept of scales and tonality by creating a song based on a major scale.

Procedure

Before using a scale to write a song, students should practice building scales by use of whole and half steps. To do this, students must have a basic knowledge of whole steps and half steps, and of sharps and flats. Using a keyboard that everyone can see, the teacher should guide students (starting on many different notes) to build the scales as follows:

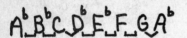   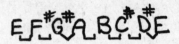

— = Whole Step

∨ = Half Step

These scales should also be written on the staff before adapting them to song writing. After a key and scale has been selected (begin with an easy one) students may write their song using a time signature and length suggested by the teacher, or choosing their own time signature and number of measures. The teacher should ask students to begin on the first note of the scale and end on that note, explaining tonality and the home tone. After the compositions have been completed, the teacher may play them or allow students to play their own compositions if they are capable.

Evaluation

Students will enjoy hearing their compositions played before the class, and constructive criticism should probably be offered at this time. Students may want to vote on their favorite composition or suggest things that they liked about a particular composition. The teacher may evaluate the mechanics of compositions (sharps, flats, time signatures, rhythms, bar lines, etc.) after the papers have been collected.

CREATING AN ORIENTAL ACCOMPANIMENT

Students will improve their creative ability and concept of oriental music by using wood blocks, sticks, finger cymbals, and a gong to create an accompaniment to an oriental song.

Procedure

Students may use an oriental song that they have sung in class or one based on a pentatonic scale that they have created. Perhaps the teacher could arrange a listening lesson to precede this activity for students to listen to oriental music and discover what instruments are used. The list will probably include woodblocks, sticks, finger cymbals, and a gong. Using these (or other) instruments selected by the students, an accompaniment should be written for the song:

This is a simple accompaniment using instruments to play on certain beats throughout the song, with the gong being played only at the beginning and end. Later students may find the total number of measures in the song and write an accompaniment where the measures are not alike each time.

Evaluation

Students may evaluate their own accompaniments with the guidance of the teacher. The accompaniment should always be kept in the background and enhance the melody. If it is too loud (or too busy) certain instruments may be discarded or played less. The teacher may evaluate students as they choose instruments from a recording and as they cooperate to develop an accompaniment. The accompaniment may be played several times, with different students playing the instruments each time as the teacher evaluates playing skills.

CREATING A MELODY ON THE RECORDER

Students will improve their creative ability by creating a melody on a recorder.

Procedure

During a unit on recorders the teacher may ask students to create a melody. This may be done as a homework assignment or students could be allotted class time to prepare their compositions. If students are expected to notate their compositions on staff paper, they must be kept simple; but if students are expected to play the composition for the class, more elaborate creations should be produced. The teacher should decide if students need practice in notation or if the composition itself is the final goal and present the assignment accordingly. A day should be set aside when students will perform their compositions for the class.

Evaluation

Evaluation will take place on the day that students perform their compositions for the class. The teacher should take into consideration students' playing skill, the length of their composition, the difficulty of the piece, and the total effect. Also, students should be evaluated according to their individual abilities, since some are not as able to perform and create as well as others.

DRAMATIZING A STORY

Students will improve their creative ability by using a folk song or ballad and dramatizing the story.

Procedure

This is a creative activity involving movement, drama and dance. Any ballad or folk song may be used, such as "John Henry,"

"Davy Crocket," or "Tom Dooley." The class should sing the ballad until they become familiar with the music, words, and story, and then plan a dramatization of the story. Characters may be chosen and suggestions for staging, movement and dances may be made until plans are completed. A final performance should be given (perhaps for another class), using scenery, a chorus to sing the song, costumes, and actions.

Evaluation

The teacher should stress cooperation as students work together to plan this activity. If many ideas are presented a vote may be needed to decide which way the performance will be given. The teacher may also evaluate students during the final performance on singing, dancing and/or acting abilities.

CREATING A DANCE

Students will improve their creative ability by creating a dance.

Procedure

Students should have had many experiences moving to music using steps, hops, skips, turns, claps, and other movements before attempting to create a dance. This is an excellent opportunity to use a pop record that has been brought from home by a student. Usually the beats will go in sets of four and the class may work together to create steps in a dance, or in small groups, in pairs, or individually. Students may wish to record their dance on paper using abbreviations in the explanation of movements to counts.

BK—Bend knees
SF—Snap fingers
SL—Step to the left
SR—Step to the right
R —Right
L —Left
K —Kick
J —Jump
C —Clap

1	2	3	4	
BK	BK	BK	BK	(For Eight Counts)

1	2	3	4	
BK	BK	BK	BK	
SF	SF	SF	SF	(For Eight Counts)

1	2	3	4	
L	R	L	R	(Walk Forward)

1	2	3	4	
R	L	R	L	(Walk Backward)

1	2	3	4
J	C	J	C

1	2	3	4	
L	R	L	R	(Walk Forward)

1	2	3	4	
R	L	R	L	(Walk Backward)

1	2	3	4
J	C	J	C

(Begin sequence again and continue to end of record.)

Evaluation

Students should be evaluated during the discussion period when the dance is created to make sure every student is participating and offering suggestions. The teacher may help shy students by asking them directly what they think and offering a choice of two ideas if they still can't find an original answer; for example, "Johnny, should we have another step, clap, step, clap, or should we go back to the beginning?" Next students should be evaluated on motor skills and learning the dance. Some students will learn this very quickly and others may never be able to perform the entire dance without mistakes. For this reason the teacher should note individual performances and give encouragement when individual students have improved their own previous efforts. Finally, evaluation will be made after the dance has been created and the steps learned when a final performance is given either for the class or on a special program.

SETTING A POEM TO MUSIC

Students will improve their creative ability by setting a poem
to music.

Procedure

There are many ways in which a poem may be set to music
following definite steps in the creation of the music.

METHOD ONE

1. Choose a subject: (Winter)

2. Ask for a sentence about winter:
     (Winter comes with snow and ice)

3. Ask for a second sentence—clap the first sentence on the
   beat and continue to the second. If the beats don't fit it
   may be necessary to rearrange, add, or remove words.

> Winter cómes with snów and íce
> It móans and blóws so cóld

4. Continue as for step three for the third line.

> Winter cómes with snów and íce
> It móans and blóws so cóld
> We púll our cóats aróund us tíght

5. Now ask for words that rhyme with cold and make a list—
   (fold, bold, gold, hold, sold, told). Finish the last line ending with a word that rhymes with cold.

> Winter comes with snow and ice;
> It moans and blows so cold.
> We pull our coats around us tight
> And wade the drifts so bold.

> It is also possible to rhyme lines 1 with 3 and 2 with 4,
> or 1 with 2 and 3 with 4.

6. Taking each line separately, ask a volunteer to sing and make up a melody for line one. Everyone then sings line one and a new volunteer sings a melody for line two. Continue until the entire song has a melody. The teacher may make suggestions along the way if students are having trouble.

METHOD TWO

After choosing a poem with simple rhythms, the class should follow these steps to create a melody:

1. Write the words under the treble clef and discuss the meaning and the mood of the words.

2. Speak the words in unison to find the rhythm.

3. Find and mark the most heavily accented words.

4. Place barlines in front of the most heavily accented words.

5. Find a melody for the first line (students sing or play on an instrument).

6. Sing the chosen melody several times.

7. Write numbers, syllables, or letter names under the words.

8. Continue to the end of the poem.

9. Translate numbers or syllable names to notation.

10. Harmonize the melody on the piano or the autoharp.[7]

METHOD THREE

1. Write a melody on staff paper.

2. Play the melody and revise.

3. Write words to fit the melody.

---

[7]Robert E. Nye and Bjornar Bergethon, *Basic Music for Classroom Teachers* (Englewood Cliffs: Prentice-Hall Inc., 1964), p. 129.

METHOD FOUR

1. Write a poem.

I love the sea and the ocean blue.

2. Write rhythms under the words.

I love the sea and the ocean blue.

3. Divide into measures.

I love the | sea and the | ocean | blue.

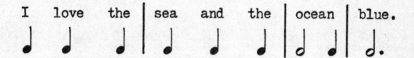

4. Place notes on the staff in a melody.

Children will need guidance when placing notes on the staff, particularly with regard to melodic direction and the avoidance of large skips. The composition should be played as the students make evaluations in order to improve their compositions.

Evaluation

Whichever method is used to create the melody of the poem, the evaluation should be conducted in the same manner. Students and the teacher should evaluate the composition together considering the following questions:

1. Does the music fit the words?
2. Do the phrases sound as if they belong together?
3. Is there a good ending?
4. Are the skips too large to sing?
5. Are the phrases too much alike or so different that they do not belong together?
6. Is the total effect good?

The melody may be changed in any area where a weakness is detected by the students.

CREATING HAIKU POETRY

Students will improve their creative ability by writing Haiku poetry.

Procedure

The teacher may begin this activity by writing several Haiku poems on the board and reading them to the class. By hearing and observing these poems, the class may discover some of the following facts about Haiku poetry. As students discover a fact, the teacher should list it on the board and then tell the students the facts that they did not find by discovery:

1. There are three lines.
2. Complete sentences are seldom found.
3. The first line is short, the second is longer and the third is short again.
4. Descriptive words are used.
5. Haiku poems often deal with nature.
6. Line one contains five syllables, line two contains seven syllables, and line three contains five syllables.

Following these rules students may try to create a Haiku poem either as a class or individually:

> Snowflakes softly fall,
> Wonderland of white glistens,
> Quiet magic land.

The teacher may guide the class by encouraging the use of descriptive words ("How does it look?", "How would you feel?", "List ten words to describe.").

Evaluation

The teacher may determine students' understanding of Haiku poetry from individual poems written by the students. These poems should follow all the rules presented at the beginning of the class even though the quality may be poor. Students should be able to write more descriptive poems of better quality with teacher guidance and their own experience.

CREATING A TWELVE TONE COMPOSITION

Students will improve their creative ability and concept of the tone row by creating a composition based upon a tone row.

Procedure

The teacher should prepare students for this activity by discussing different scales which have a "do" or "home tone." The Austrian, Schoenberg, may then be introduced, explaining that he wanted to make a new pitch organization, a tone row, without a "do." Twelve students may then take twelve chromatic resonator bells and stand in order. The chromatic scale will be heard as each student plays his bell in the correct order. Students then may mix up their order and play again, sounding a tone row. If major thirds or parts of familiar scales are heard, students should exchange places until no familiar scale organization can be detected. Students may then take a familiar song (such as "Jingle Bells") and use the rhythm for the melody of the tone row. The song begins with the first person, then the second and so forth until the entire row is used to the rhythm of "Jingle Bells." When the final tone is sounded the row begins again until the entire rhythm of "Jingle Bells" has been completed. No tone may be reused until the entire row is finished. If two sets of bells are available one set may be used to play the new melody and the other set to play chords (three or four bells together in the order of the original row) for an accompaniment. Students may experiment further by playing their

row to the rhythm backward (retrograde) or in a mirror image
(inversion) going up a fourth if the original went down a fourth,
down a second if the original went up a second, and inverting all
the intervals.

Evaluation

The teacher may present this lesson and later evaluate students when the activity is used again. Students should be able to
tell and demonstrate to the teacher certain facts about the tone
row. Learnings that should have been achieved include:

1. Schoenberg is responsible for the tone row.

2. He wanted to make a pitch organization without a "do" or
   "home tone."

3. If any major chords or familiar scale patterns are heard the
   row should be changed.

4. No tone can be reused until all of the row has been used.

5. Tones may be played together as chords in the order of the
   original row.

6. Retrograde is the original row played backward.

7. Inversion is a mirror-like effect inverting the intervals.

8. Students should be able to go through the procedure of
   creating a song using a tone row.

CREATIVITY WITH FORM

Students will improve their creative ability and concept of
form by creating compositions in different forms.

Procedure

Students should be familiar with various forms used in music,
such as binary (AB), ternary (ABA), Rondo (ABACA), fugue,
theme and variation, tone poem, or through composed. The

teacher may use simple forms in the lower grades and more difficult ones for older students. Any type of composition may be used to create a song in a given form (electronic composition, a sound tape, an instrumental, a song with words, or a rhythmic or percussion composition). The form should be determined and the procedure varied for each type of composition created.

Evaluation

The teacher may evaluate students on their cooperative effort to create the composition, the results of the composition, their performance skills, and their ability to apply a particular form to the composition. Students should have had previous experience creating each type of composition before trying to apply it to a particular form.

Chapter 6

Teaching Sight Reading Through Singing and Playing Instruments

Activities in this section will deal with methods and techniques designed to improve students' ability in sight reading. Exercises will begin with simple melodic diagrams and rhythmic exercises and advance to more complex activities to aid students in reading music.

PREPARING FOR MUSIC READING

Students will prepare for music reading by participating in various musical activities.

Procedure

Before students attempt to sight read they should have many other experiences with music. Some of these include:

1. Singing many songs by rote
2. Listening to music and discovering
   A. Tempo
   B. Mood
   C. Timbre
   D. Dynamics
   E. Rhythm
   F. Melodic characteristics
   G. Form

3. Moving to music (skip, run, walk, hop, slide)

4. Creating simple songs

5. Playing rhythm and melodic instruments

6. Observing printed music

Evaluation

Progress in these areas involves students' readiness for sight reading. Each of these activities should be evaluated in individual ways determining when a class is ready to begin sight reading experiences. When sight reading is introduced it should begin with easy activities dealing with melodic direction or simple rhythms. If students cannot succeed at first the teacher should review more of the seven activities listed above and try again later. If sight reading activities are started at a simple level dealing with one concept at a time, students should succeed after several attempts. Only intelligent practice can assure improvement, so the teacher should continue daily efforts in this area.

MELODIC HAND MOVEMENT

Students will improve their concept of melodic direction by moving their hands to the contour of a melody.

Procedure

Students in the lower grades should have many experiences moving their hands in the direction of the melody (up, down, or stay the same). At first this may be limited to only portions of the songs, as the teacher demonstrates to the students asking, "Did the melody go up or down or stay the same?" or "Did you hear steps or skips?" Students then may be asked to join the teacher in singing the song and showing the melodic direction with their hands. By using this activity students have a visual aid to help with the concept of melodic direction (up, down, or same) and movement (steps or skips).

Evaluation

The teacher may evaluate students as they move their hands to the music. At first students may suddenly reach too high or too low and, as the melody continues, they cannot stretch far enough. The teacher should caution children about this and soon they will correspond their movements with the melody. They will move their hands up or down only a short distance unless a large skip is sounded or unless the music goes very high or very low. Students may follow the hand movements of the teacher as a song is introduced and sung in class. With the teacher as a guide, the students will grasp the concept rapidly, and later the teacher can evaluate when he/she is not involved in leading the class.

DRAWING PICTURE MELODIES

Students will improve their sight reading ability by drawing a picture of a melody.

Procedure

As the teacher sings (or plays) a song that has a simple melodic direction, students may first show with their hands "how the melody goes." One student may then come to the board, or each student may have a paper at his desk to draw a picture of the melody using dashes, connected lines, or curves. Before students are expected to draw a melodic line individually, there should have been class sessions where the teacher drew "pictures" of melodies. Using the first phrase of "Twinkle Twinkle Little Star," examples of such melodic picture might be as follows:

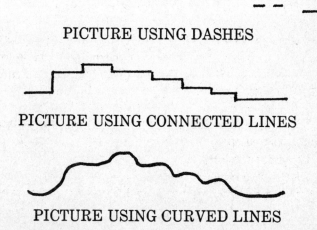

PICTURE USING DASHES

PICTURE USING CONNECTED LINES

PICTURE USING CURVED LINES

Evaluation

The teacher should compare the original music with the students' pictures. If the skips, steps, repetition, and melodic direction correspond with the song, the student has a basic awareness of melodic direction. This idea may later be transferred to the printed page as students look at the notes to determine the melodic direction (up, down, or same) and movement (step or skip).

PLAYING MELODIC DIAGRAMS

Students will improve their sight reading ability and concept of melodic direction by reading and playing diagrams of melodies.

Procedure

The teacher should have a set of melody bells available and ten melodic diagrams on the board that all of the students can see:

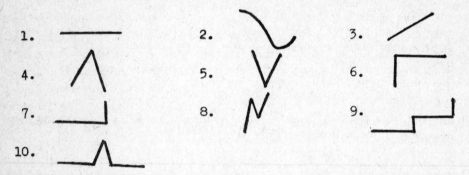

Students should come to the bells one at a time, choose one of the diagrams and play it on the bells (as example nine stays the same, goes up, stays the same and goes up). Students at their desks try to identify the correct example and the person who is successful then plays another example to be identified.

A variation of this activity provides practice in ear training. Melody bells are still used but no diagrams are listed on the board. A student plays a simple melody and chooses another student to draw a diagram of the melody on the board. If he cannot draw the example, it is played again and another student is chosen to draw the diagram. The student who can draw the example plays the next melody (always keeping the melody simple) and the game continues.

Evaluation

The teacher may evaluate students by their ability to play and identify the diagrams listed on the board. Although examples may be played differently by students (some may go higher or lower or stay on one note longer) the general direction of the melody should be distinct. After students are able to perform and identify these simple patterns, longer and more difficult diagrams may be used.

READING MUSIC WITH PICTURES

Students will begin reading rhythms by using pictures of instruments and standard notation of rests.

Procedure

Before reading rhythms using standard notation, students may find it easier to use pictures of the instruments. The rest should be introduced to use with this type of picture notation. Students may be chosen to play each instrument while the remainder of the class is assigned to a type of instrument and clap when it is to be played. First, the example may be played one line at a time and then with the instruments together as each person repeats the example four times.

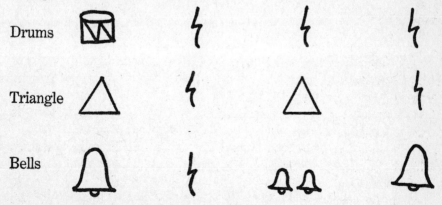

Later, as standard notation is introduced, instrument symbols can still be used:

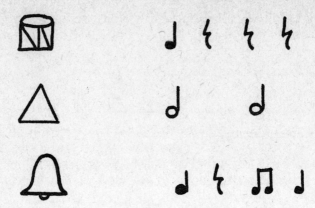

Evaluation

Students may be evaluated by their ability to read and play the examples correctly. If one section is having difficulty the teacher may have everyone clap or play that part. Lack of coordination may pose a problem for some students who will need extra practice to achieve success. When students are able to perform their part alone, combinations of instruments should be tried together until everyone can play together staying on their own part.

READING LINE NOTATION

Students will improve their ability to read rhythms and their concept of notation by using line notation.

Procedure

The teacher should have several examples of line notation written on the board:

1. __ __ __ __   2. __ __ __ __ __
3. _ _ _ _ __ __   4. ___ _ _ __ _
5. _____ _ _ __   6. _____
7. _____ _ _   8. __ __ __ ___

The class may clap through all of the examples to make sure that everyone understands how to read and perform line notation. The teacher should then ask a student to choose an example and clap it. The remainder of the class should try to guess which example was clapped. The person who identifies the example correctly then becomes the leader and claps a new example to be identified.

Evaluation

As the class claps all of the examples together, the teacher should listen and **repeat** those with which the students seem to have difficulty. The lesson should not be continued until all of the examples can be clapped correctly. Individual students may then be evaluated as they become leaders and clap examples from the board. The class should also be evaluated as they identify the correct examples. The teacher could also use this as a written test, clapping the examples to be identified on paper by the students. The papers can then be collected for a more accurate evaluation.

VERBAL NOTE VALUES

Students will improve their concept of rhythmic notation by associating note values with words or syllables.

Procedure

The teacher may use types of motions or syllable association to aid students in reading rhythms. There are several standard methods, or teachers may use a combination of these or invent a new system that works well within the framework of their professional setting.

METHOD ONE

Ta	♩	Ti-ti	♫	Triple-ti	♫
Ti-di-ti-di	♬	Ta-a	♩	Ta-a-a	♩.
Ta-a-a-a	𝅝	Ta-ti-ta-ti	♩ ♪♩ ♪	Ti-di-ti-di	♩. ♫♩. ♫
Ti, ti-di	♩♫	Ti-di, ti	♫♩	Rest	𝄽

METHOD TWO

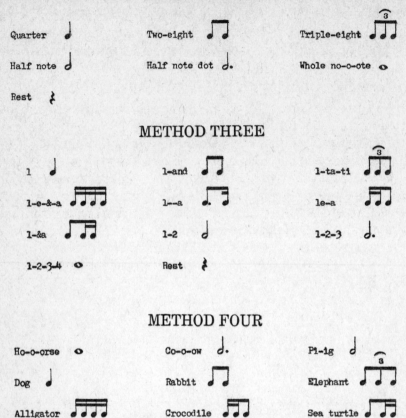

Each of these methods are devised for sight reading so that measures can be read chanting words or syllables in the correct rhythms. Any system may be used that works well, but the teacher should strive for Method Three where counts are used. Although each count was started with the number one in Method Three, they should be adapted to the count that falls in the measure (1, 2, 3, 4, 5, and 6).

Evaluation

The teacher may judge the success of the method being used by the students' ability to clap rhythmic patterns. If students are having difficulty, the teacher may explain the method that is being used again, review simpler patterns, change the method of reading rhythms, or find additional activities to reinforce the concept.

RHYTHM FLASH CARDS

Students will improve their ability to read rhythms by using flash cards.

Procedure

The teacher should prepare several sets of flash cards made of three inch by four inch poster board. Each of these cards should have a rhythmic pattern printed on the front with the answer written on the back in terms that the students can understand (only one method needs to be used on the back).

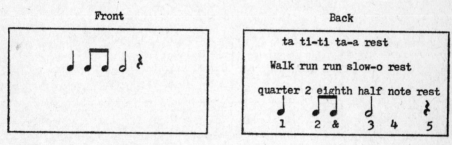

The students work in small groups with one student showing the card and the others clapping the rhythm. The leader can tell if the group is clapping the rhythm correctly by looking at the back of the card. When all of the cards are completed a new leader may show them or a contest can be held giving the card to the person who first claps it correctly. The person with the most cards at the end of the contest wins.

Evaluation

This is an individualized activity where the teacher may walk about the room observing different groups. The leader must evaluate students as they clap the rhythms by referring to the back of the card. Later the teacher may evaluate students by holding up the flash cards and having individual students or the complete class clap the rhythms together. This is an excellent reinforcement activity if students are having difficulty sight reading rhythms from the board.

CLAPPING NUMBERS

Students will improve their sight reading ability by reading numbers from a chart.

Procedure

This is an excellent opportunity to use a pop record (in duple meter) brought to school by a student. The following chart should be made on the board or on a large piece of poster board:

1	2	3	4	5	6	7	8
1		3		5		7	
1		3		5		7	8
1		3	4		6	7	8
			4	5	6	7	
1	2					7	8
	2		4	5			8
		3			6		8

Groups of students should be assigned to rows on the chart. Row one is clapped on all 8 beats, row two on beats 1, 3, 5 and 7, etc. The teacher may wish to have students clap rows one through eight together before assigning group rows. As the record is played everyone should count in eights and clap on the correct counts in their row.

Evaluation

This activity requires a great deal of concentration as well as coordination. At first, the teacher may assign everyone to a particular row until students can clap together with the record. The next two groups could be used on different rows. As students improve, more groups on different rows should be used until eight groups can clap all of the rows together.

CHOOSING RHYTHM PATTERNS

Students will reinforce their ability to read notated rhythmic patterns by choosing which pattern was clapped.

Procedure

The teacher should list ten examples on the board using four count rhythmic patterns.

The class should be divided into two teams, A and B. The first person on team A claps an example and the first person on team B tries to identify the example clapped. The first person on team B then claps an example for the first person on team A to identify. If the person can identify the example his team gets a point, but if he cannot, the other team gets the point. An example clapped incorrectly gives the other team a point. The next people on teams A and B then come forward and the game continues until everyone has had a turn and the team with the most points wins the game.

Evaluation

The teacher may evaluate individual students as they clap rhythmic patterns and identify examples clapped. If students are having difficulty, the examples should be clapped by the class collectively before continuing. If students still cannot succeed, examples should be simplified to a degree that will insure student success. More difficult rhythmic patterns may be used in upper grades using sixteenth notes and rests, dotted rhythms, and syncopation. The teacher must always evaluate carefully to determine if students are ready to deal with more difficult rhythms.

READING FROM A TWO LINE STAFF

Students will improve their sight reading ability by using a two line staff and the syllables sol and mi.

Procedure

When introducing young students to sight reading, the teacher may begin by using a two line staff and the syllables sol and mi:

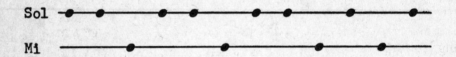

Next rhythms should be added:

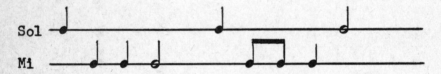

Finally words are included in the examples:

Evaluation

Students should first master the ability to read the syllables sol and mi from a two line staff before adding rhythms to the task. If the rhythms are added too quickly students will not grasp the basic concept of music reading. When students are able to handle many rhythms reading the two syllables, the next dimension of words may be added. New syllables and lines on the staff may be added gradually until students can sight read any song using simple interval skips and rhythms. Only practice and constant reinforcement in this area will assure success. There may be times when the teacher can detect little if any improvement, and it is important not to become discouraged and discontinue the sight reading program.

METHODS OF SIGHT READING

Students will improve their music reading skill by sight reading from the board.

Procedure

The teacher should prepare charts or write simple songs on the board with the difficulty of the songs depending on the ability of the students. Beginning students should start with two syllable songs (sol and mi) and gradually go on to more difficult songs by adding the syllables la, do re, ti, and fa in that order. (The appropriate number may also be used instead of the syllable.) Students should clap the rhythm of the charted song, sing the syllables or numbers in rhythm, and finally sing the song using the correct words and rhythms. All of this should be done with no instrumental help and as little assistance as possible from the teacher.

If the teacher prepares the song on a chart, it can be stored away for later use. These songs can then be used along with a graduated sight reading series when extra help and reinforcement are indicated. Songs may be charted using only the words, syllables, and rhythms; or they may be charted on a staff.

METHOD ONE

Although syllables have been used in this example numbers may be used instead if students sight read by the number method.

METHOD TWO

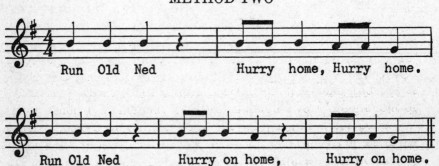

Evaluation

The teacher must evaluate the students' work by listening as they sight read. The teacher may find it necessary to sing along with students in certain parts of the song in order to keep them from floundering. If certain skips or passages are difficult the group should work on them separately. When the sight reading material seems to be too difficult the teacher should provide shorter and easier songs. Such charts as the ones described are necessary to supplement a standard sight reading series. After evaluation, the teacher must decide where extra help is needed and provide the extra materials and help that are necessary. If the school cannot afford a regular sight reading series, the teacher can develop one through the use of sight reading charts described in this activity.

SIGHT READING GAME

Students will improve their sight reading ability by singing examples and guessing which example was sung.

Procedure

The teacher should list five to ten short examples on the board where all of the students can see them. The examples should be sung by all of the students together using syllables or numbers. A leader is then chosen to sing one of the examples on "la" while the class tries to guess which example was sung. The person who identifies the correct example becomes the leader and the game continues. Examples that might be drawn on the board include the following:

Evaluation

True sight reading in this activity takes place as students read the examples together using syllables or numbers. The teacher should evaluate students, making notes of which intervals are most difficult and giving as little help as possible. When the class begins to have difficulty the teacher may have them stop, comprehend the correct intervals, and begin again. In addition, students may be helped as the teacher joins in order to get them back on the correct note and pitch. As soon as they are carrying the melody again, the teacher's voice should drop out.

Beginning students may need a great deal of help carrying the melody, but as they advance the teacher should give little help and stop them to find the correct interval if they get lost. The teacher may further evaluate students as they become leaders and sing examples individually (checking tone quality, sharp or flat notes, ability to carry the tune, and breathing). This could also be used as a test where the teacher sings the examples and the students write on paper which examples were performed.

READING FROM TREBLE
AND BASS CLEF

Students will improve their concept of high and low, and treble and bass clef by reading music from both the treble and the bass clefs.

Procedure

The teacher should introduce the treble and bass clef signs corresponding them to low and high tones. Students may then name low and high instruments found in the music room.

Low	High
1. Bass Marimba	1. Melody Bells
2. Bass Drum	2. Recorders
3. Tympani	3. Tambourine
4. Low Notes on Piano	4. High Notes on Piano

After several students are chosen to play low and high instruments, the teacher should write a simple example on the board using treble and bass clefs:

Students with low instruments play the bass clef and students with high instruments play the treble clef. Some instrument players will only watch the rhythms (drums or tambourine) while others must play the notes and rhythms (Marimba, piano, bells, or recorder). When these students have played the example correctly, they should give their instruments to others in the class. The example is played again with different students.

Evaluation

Students must be familiar with rhythms, notes, and where the notes are found on the instruments before this activity can be performed successfully. Examples to be played must be kept simple, using only one or two different notes at first, and later advancing to longer and more difficult examples. At first, the teacher may introduce the treble and bass clefs using only low and high rhythm instruments in order that students do not have to read the notes, only the rhythms.

RHYTHM MATCH

Students will improve their ability to read rhythms by matching rhythms to songs.

Procedure

The teacher should prepare a paper to be handed to students containing examples similar to the following:

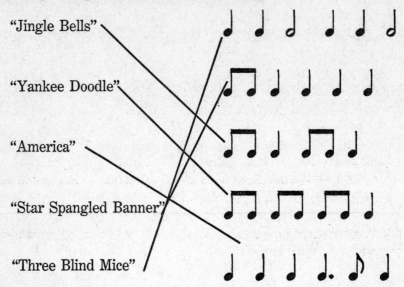

The students must match the correct rhythm to the song. Although only a few examples have been listed above, the teacher may list a full page of song names and beginning rhythms. A variation of this activity would be to list the first measure or two on the staff so that students must read both the notes and the rhythms in order to match the songs to the correct staff.

Evaluation

The teacher may evaluate students by grading their papers. If students do poorly on the activity the teacher may review these songs, bringing attention to the rhythms of the beginning phrases as they are read from the students' books. If students do well on the activity the teacher may prepare another sheet using more difficult songs. In most classes a few students do very well and a few do very poorly, with the majority of students achieving an average level. The teacher must develop lessons directed to this major group, but special activities should be provided for high achievers and special help should be given to low achievers.

SIGHT READING MYSTERY

Students will improve their sight reading ability by reading a familiar song and guessing the name of the song.

Procedure

The beginning phrase of a very familiar song should be notated on the board. Students first clap the rhythm, then say the syllables (or numbers) in rhythm, and finally sing the phrase using the syllables or numbers. After singing, students may try to guess the name of the song. Some simple songs that are appropriate for this activity include:

"This Old Man"	"Bingo"
"Twinkle Twinkle Little Star"	"Skip to My Lou"
"Hot Cross Buns"	"Silent Night"
"Jingle Bells"	"If You're Happy and You
"Yankee Doodle"	Know It"
"Paw Paw Patch"	"Old MacDonald"

Evaluation

The teacher should evaluate students on their ability to clap the rhythm, to say the syllables or numbers, and to sing the song using syllables or numbers. Usually only the first phrase of these songs will be needed to identify the song. (The entire song may be used if necessary.) To avoid having a student call out the name of the song and negate the sight reading experience for the other students, the teacher may have the students raise their hand if they know the name of the song. After reading through the song three times (additional hands should be raised each time), a student may be selected to call out the name of the song. If no student can name the song after three tries, the teacher may divide the class in half and let one side sing and the other side listen and then reverse sides. If the students still do not know the answer, the teacher may sing the phrase using syllables or numbers. By this time, the students usually have guessed the song. Students look forward to this type of musical reading activity with familiar songs more than using the usual sight reading books with unfamiliar songs. However, it is still important that such a continuous program with sight reading books be used regularly, with guessing activities (such as described above) used to add variety.

PROCEDURES FOR SIGHT READING

Students will improve their ability to sight read by reading many songs in a graduated music reading program.

Procedure

To assure success in sight reading, the teacher should provide a continuous daily program containing many songs for students to read. This is not a short term objective that can be measured weekly, but a long term objective that will produce gradual improvement. It is important to begin with individualized concepts in music reading, such as rhythm and pitch, then use both rhythm and pitch together and finally these together with the addition of expressive elements. To guide students in the sight reading process the teacher may wish to use one of the following outlines:

PROCEDURES FOR SIGHT READING[8]

1. Look at the meter signature and conduct a few measures in rhythm.
2. Scan the words in rhythm.
3. Look at the key signature. Establish "do" and then think the starting pitch from "do."
4. Think through the part.
5. Sing the part.
6. Hear the part for accuracy.

PRESENTING A NEW SONG FOR READING

1. Introductory remarks—Motivate students

2. Look at the kinds of notes
   a. Chant rhythms
   b. Read words in rhythm

---

[8]Based on personal correspondence between Mrs. Claudine Terry, Teacher at Northeast Missouri State University in the Fine Arts Department, and the writer, July, 1974.

3. Look at the pitches
   a. Look at the first and last pitch
   b. Look for familiar patterns
   c. Look for hard skips

4. Give key and practice passages
   a. Do, re, mi, fa, sol, fa, mi, re, do
   b. Do, mi, sol, do, sol, mi, do

5. Conduct the class and sing the song using numbers or syllables and then the words

Evaluation

The teacher should evaluate students daily to determine their success in individual song experiences. Substantial improvement, however, must be evaluated over a long term period. When students seem to be making no improvement, it is important not to become discouraged and discontinue the sight reading program. It may be necessary to return to easier material at these times and progress to more difficult songs gradually again.

Chapter 7

Activities for Teaching Tone Matching and Phrasing

Activities in this section will deal with methods and techniques designed to improve students' singing and playing skills. Concepts of high, low, skip, and step will be studied through tone matching and singing games to aid the out-of-tune singer. Form will be presented using activities of phrase identification and diagramming. Proper singing habits, playing skills, and good attitudes toward music will be strengthened as students are involved in enjoyable activities to further their knowledge and skills.

HELPING THE OUT-OF-TUNE SINGER

The teacher may help out-of-tune singers by following these suggestions:[9]

1. Encourage *every* child to sing.
2. Insist that every child give his complete attention when the music is being played or sung.
3. Seat out-of-tune singers near good singers.
4. Stress light singing, never harsh singing.
5. Be generous with praise and encouragement.
6. Individual work is a must.
7. Use many tone matching games.

---

[9]Phyllis R. Gelineau, *Experiences in Music.* (New York: McGraw-Hill Book Company, 1976). Used with permission of McGraw-Hill Book Company, p. 12.

Evaluation

Success will not be immediate when working on the problem of matching pitch. When students improve, or do match a pitch, the teacher should be generous with praise and encouragement. One (or even a few) successful experiences will not solve the students' problems. Following the suggestions listed above will aid students in their struggle to match pitch and to sing in tune.

HIGH AND LOW, STEP AND SKIP

Students will improve their tone matching ability by singing songs that reinforce concepts of high, low, step, and skip.

Procedure

Many songs and phrases are needed to help students who have a problem matching pitch. These songs should be easy and should deal with the concepts of high, low, step, or skip. Short phrases to be echoed are also excellent:

Evaluation

The teacher can evaluate students only by listening as they match pitches and sing these songs or phrases. For this reason students should sing individually so that the teacher can make an accurate evaluation. At first students may be shy and reluctant to sing alone. When this happens the teacher may start with small groups, then use duets, and finally have students sing individually. It is helpful to keep a note card on each student, recording individual progress in the area of tone matching. The teacher could also tape students' performances to keep as a future reference.

GUESS WHAT I HAVE

Students will improve their ability to match pitch by playing a game called "Guess What I Have."

Procedure

The teacher should have several small articles that can be hidden in her/his hands. A clue may be given, such as "This is something that you have in your desks." Then the teacher sings:

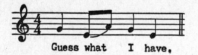

Students take turns guessing:

When students have guessed the wrong answer the teacher sings:

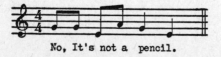

When a student is correct the teacher sings:

The object is then shown to the class and a new object is held as a clue is given and the game continues.

Evaluation

This is an activity that students will enjoy and it will motivate them to sing individually. As they sing the teacher should listen to hear if they are matching the tune correctly. If the singer is out-of-tune the teacher may ask the student to repeat the phrase. This game should be fun and the teacher should avoid taking a lot of time to stop and work on individual problems. These problems can be noted during the game and individual help given at a later time.

SINGING MELODIC PATTERNS

Students will improve their ability to match tones by singing a short melodic pattern as they leave the music room.

Procedure

When the music period is over the teacher may end the session with a tone matching game. The teacher should choose a short melodic pattern using numbers or syllables, such as one of the following:

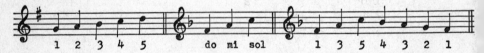

The teacher sings first and each student must repeat the melodic pattern. If the student is successful he may leave the room. If not, he should be seated as the teacher continues listening to each student. There may be several students who were not able to match the pitch by the end of the period. The teacher may listen to them individually again or sing each pitch of the pattern separately as the students echo the note together. When they have sung the pattern the second time they may leave the music room.

Evaluation

This activity should be done quickly with no pause between students as they sing the melodic pattern. The teacher may evaluate students immediately by listening and then saying "Go" if they are successful or "Stay" if they sing the pattern incorrectly. When the out-of-tune singer tries the second time, the teacher may offer such suggestions as "Try to get a little higher." or "No, that's too high." These students may not be able to sing the pattern correctly the second time either, but they should be dismissed with encouragement. "That's better," "You're improving," or "Fine, I'll see you Monday," are good phrases to use as students leave the room.

PAUSING BEFORE THE FINAL PITCH

Students will improve their tonal memory and ability to sing a given pitch by counting to ten before singing the last note of a song.

Procedure

The class should sing a well-known song, stopping after the singing of the next to the last note. The teacher then counts aloud to ten and the students try to sing the last note of the song. This will improve students' concentration, tonal memory, and singing ability.

Evaluation

The teacher should listen carefully as students try to sing the last note of the song. If they are not able to perform the task the teacher may have them sing the song without hesitating before the singing of the last note, or count fewer numbers than ten. If students are able to perform the task the teacher may stop students several times in the song, count to ten, and hear if they can continue on the correct pitch.

TONE MATCHING GAME

Students will improve their ability to match pitches by playing
a tone matching game.

Procedure

The class should be divided into two groups and corners of the
room be designated as bases. After a score keeper is appointed the
teacher plays a short melodic pattern on the piano or bells. The
person "at bat" reproduces what was played by singing each pitch
accurately. If he succeeds he advances to the next base but if he is
wrong it counts as an "out" for his team. After three players strike
out the next team goes up to bat. As students' ability progresses,
the patterns should become more difficult.

Evaluation

Students may help evaluate the other team by acting as um-
pires and calling outs when the pattern is reproduced incorrectly.
The teacher may make notes on students as they sing the melodic
patterns. Keep the notes in the music files. These files will indicate
which students need additional help with tone matching.

HIGH LOW GAME

Students will improve their concept of low and high and their
tone matching ability by repeating their names in low and high
voices.

Procedure

When students are having difficulty matching pitch because
they cannot make their voices go high or low the teacher may use
the following activity. A high and low pitch may be designated by
the teacher, or students may find their own "high" or "low" pitch.
When calling roll at the beginning of class, the teacher may ask
students to answer in a high or low voice. Every other student
could be high or low or each student could say their name twice,
once in a high voice and once in a low voice.[10]

---

[10]Phyllis R. Gelineau, *Experiences in Music*. (New York: McGraw-Hill Book Company,
1976). Used with permission of McGraw-Hill Book Company, p.13.

Evaluation

The teacher must evaluate the students as they sing, making notes to be used for later reference and additional help. If a high and low pitch have been designated, students should match those pitches. If the teacher is working on the concept of high and low with students who cannot match pitch, these students may find their own pitches by trying to sing their name in high and low voices. If a student has difficulty, the teacher may stop and give additional help by asking the student to reach high as he sings and make a high buzz like a fast car, or growl low like a bear or sound low and sad. Use any suggestions of low and high sounds to help students associate familiar circumstances, activities, or sounds.

NAME MELODIES

Students will improve their ability to match pitches by finding a melodic pattern for their name and repeating that pattern.

Procedure

Students should take turns coming to a set of melody bells in the front of the room and finding a melody for their name. The melody should not be too high or low, have difficult skips, or be very complicated. After a melody has been found, the student should play the bells and sing his name. The other students in the class then sing the melodic pattern to the student's name as he plays it on the bells. The next student comes to the bells and finds a new melody for his name as the activity continues.

Evaluation

The teacher may first evaluate the student at the bells as he creates a melody for his name. Suggestions may be offered if the melody is too high or low, has difficult skips, or if it is too complicated. This student can also be evaluated on his singing and playing skills as he sings and plays his name for the class. Finally, the class may be evaluated on their ability to sing the student's name. If the melody is sung incorrectly, students should repeat the name until the melody is performed correctly.

HIDE AND SEEK

Students will improve their ability to match pitch by playing a hide and seek singing game.

Procedure

As the teacher appoints a leader the other students imagine a place to hide. The leader sings "Where is (John)?" using a tune that has been improvised. John answers in the same tune "I'm in the desk." If he does not sing in tune, the same leader sings another tune using a different name ("Where is Mary?"). Mary answers and the game continues.

Evaluation

This is a good exercise to reinforce the concept of improvisation as well as the ability to match tones. Improvised melodies should be kept simple without using awkward skips. At first, students may find it difficult to improvise melodies, but will rely on familar tunes previously used. The teacher should encourage students to try new tunes to improve their ability to improvise. The teacher should continue the evaluation as students try to match the improvised melody. Notes may be taken on individual ability and progress or the teacher may elect to listen and evaluate the class as a whole.

PHRASE DETECTION

Students will strengthen their concept of phrase by raising their hand at the end of a phrase.

Procedure

To develop an awareness of phrases in music the teacher may begin by using nursery rhymes. Point out that there are places that make the reader feel like stopping for a minute. As the teacher recites a nursery rhyme students should be asked to listen for these places. The second time the poem is recited students should raise their hands when they feel that the words hesitate a minute. Next, a song may be sung as students raise their hands at the end of each phrase. Words in the song will help students find the phrases. After students are able to detect phrases in songs with words, the teacher may play songs without words and ask students to raise their hands when they hear the end of a phrase (when they feel like stopping for a minute or when they feel that they are at the end of one musical idea and ready to begin another). It is difficult to explain to students exactly what a phrase is. They will have to develop a feeling for phrasing which can only be done by experience in detecting phrases.

Evaluation

The teacher may evaluate students as they raise their hands to indicate the end of phrases. At first, poems or songs may be performed with exaggerated hesitation at the end of phrases. After students understand the concept of phrasing, songs and poems should be performed with natural phrasing. Some students may look around the room and follow other students as they raise their hands. To avoid this, the teacher may ask students to close their eyes as they listen. This will provide a more accurate means of evaluation.

COUNTING PHRASES

Students will improve their concept of phrasing by counting the number of phrases in a song.

Procedure

As a song is played (or sung) the students should count the number of phrases in the song. It is necessary that students first understand the concept of phrasing before trying this activity. When students tell the number of phrases in the song, there may be differences of opinion. To avoid confusion, the teacher may accept several logical answers as being "correct" and then announce which answer seems "best." This activity could also be used as a written test to evaluate students' understanding of phrasing.

Evaluation

The teacher may evaluate students as they announce the number of phrases found in the song. Since several answers may be acceptable, students should tell the number of phrases and why they think their choice is correct. The teacher should acknowledge all logical answers and then tell which answer she/he feels is best. The same problem will occur if this is used as a written examination. The teacher should be lenient in grading and accept more than one answer as "correct" if the phrasing could be felt in different ways.

DIAGRAMMING PHRASES

Students will improve their concept of phrasing by diagramming phrases.

Procedure

After students are familiar with the concept of phrasing, the teacher may guide students in drawing diagrams of phrases. This may be used with a listening example or with a song that is being sung in class. At first, the teacher may diagram several phrases showing climaxes (usually high, loud, or dissonant places):

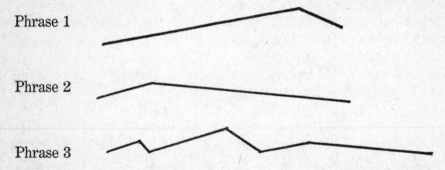

Students may try to diagram their own phrases on paper and then compare them to see if they are similar to other diagrams of the same phrase. The teacher should caution students that these are not melodic diagrams but phrasing diagrams used to show the contour of the phrase, including the climax.

Evaluation

Students may evaluate their own efforts as they compare diagrams of the same phrase. Diagrams should be similar. Therefore, if a student's diagram is completely unlike the others he will know that it is not correct. The teacher may choose what she/he feels is the best diagram and hold it up for the class to see to evaluate their own diagram. If the diagrams are all different, the teacher should realize that the students have not grasped the concept of showing phrases by diagrams. The class may then try diagramming phrases together at the chalkboard before attempting individual diagrams again.

CARD PHRASING

Students will improve their concept of phrasing by using colored cards to represent phrases.

Procedure

The teacher should have several pieces of colored cards or construction paper (about 5" x 11"). Each phrase may be represented by a certain color of card. First a song should be sung (or played) and the number of phrases determined. One student should be assigned to represent each phrase. As the song is sung again each student should come forward, select a colored card, and hold it up in order. If a phrase is repeated the same color of card must be used again:

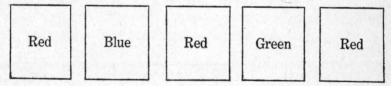

In this example a song of five phrases was performed with phrases one, three, and five alike and phrases two and four different (rondo form). This activity not only reinforces the concept of phrasing but also that of form.

Evaluation

The teacher should first evaluate students as they determine the number of phrases in the song. Suggestions may be offered if students are having trouble agreeing on the phrasing of the song. After students are assigned a phrase, the teacher should watch to see that they hold up the correct color of card. The first person may choose any color, but after that students must listen to see if their phrase is like a previous phrase or if it is different, and then select a card accordingly. After students are in order with their cards, the song may be sung again to see that all the cards match the phrasing.

SOLO PHRASES

Students will improve their concept of phrasing by singing solos on different phrases of a song.

Procedure

After a song has been sung and the phrases identified, the teacher should assign each phrase to a person in the class. As the song is performed again, each of the soloists should sing only on their phrase. If a phrase is repeated, the same person may sing it again (showing the form of the song).

Evaluation

Evaluation of phrasing will occur as students identify phrases to be sung by the soloists. As these phrases are sung, the teacher may evaluate students on their singing skills (enunciation, tone quality, breathing, and expression). Using soloists in this manner will give students an aural and visual aid to reinforce the concept of phrasing.

PERFORMING PHRASES

Students will improve their concept of phrasing by performing different actions for phrases.

Procedure

As students stand in a circle (or at their deks) a song should be sung and the phrases identified. Then the students should select actions and perform them on different phrases:

Phrase 1—Walk   (A)   Phrase 2—Clap   (B)
Phrase 3—Hop   (C)   Phrase 4—Walk   (A)

If phrases are alike, the same action should be performed (Phrases one and four). Finally, the song is performed again as students sing and do the assigned actions for the phrase.

Evaluation

Students should be evaluated as they first identify the phrases in the song. Creative efforts may then be encouraged and evaluated as students select different actions to correspond to the phrases. Finally, students should be evaluated on their performance skill as the song is sung with the actions. It may be difficult for some students to sing and do the actions at the same time. To overcome this, the song may be performed with the words and the actions separately before trying to combine them.

GOOD SINGING HABITS

Students will improve their ability to sing by reviewing a list of good singing habits before beginning a song.

Procedure

The teacher and students may work together to devise a list of good singing habits. This list should be posted somewhere in the room and reviewed occasionally. Such a list may include the following:

1. Posture
   A. Feet on the floor
   B. Sit straight but not stiff

2. Breathing
   A. Controlled continuous flow of breath
   B. Breath with diaphram muscles, not chest muscles

3. Open throat—relaxed as in a yawn

4. Good Enunciation
   A. Open mouth
   B. Stay on vowel sounds
   C. Sound final consonants

5. Good tone quality
   A. Sing "light"
   B. Do not force the tone

6. Expression
   A. Use dynamic and tempo markings
   B. Sing in phrases with feeling

7. Balance
   A. Blend voices together
   B. Have parts equal in strength
   C. Accompaniment should be softer than the melody

Evaluation

The students should review this list before beginning a song. It will not be necessary to review the list before every song, but when students are sluggish and not doing their best, this review may bring vitality back into their singing. After a song has been sung the teacher may go over the list again and discuss with the students which areas need improvement and which the students performed well.

SIT UP STRAIGHT

Students will improve their posture by singing a song to the tune of "Are You Sleeping?"

Procedure

When the class is sitting with their feet on their chairs and slumped over, the teacher may sing the following song to the tune of "Are You Sleeping?": (Composer unknown)

> Sit up straight, Sit up straight
> Never slump, Never slump
> Or you'll be a camel, yes you'll be a camel
> With a hump, with a hump.

After the class knows the words to the song they may sing it together as an opening activity to achieve good posture before continuing the class.

Evaluation

When the teacher first sings this song students will be amused and sit up very straight. Some students may think it funny to hump over even more, like the camel. If this happens, the teacher should let the students know that even though the song is funny, the meaning is serious and they need to sit straight when singing. A discussion of good posture and the reasons it is required may follow the introduction of this song.

ACTING MELODIES

Students will improve their playing skills and concept of melodic movement by playing and acting out melodies.

Procedure

Five tones should be used on the piano, bells, or xylophone and five students assigned to pretend to be these musical tones. One student should play the notes from low to high as the five students arrange themselves from low to high (squat, sit, kneel, stand, and raise hands). Another student comes to the bells and plays the five tones in a different order as students arrange themselves again in the new order. This will give students a visual aid to see if melodies go up or down or move by steps or skips. Later, more tones and students may be used to act out more difficult melodies.

Evaluation

The teacher may watch students to see that they are in the correct order (low or high) as the melody moves. Students at their seats may help in this evaluation by telling the other students to stand taller or to bend lower if the order is not correct.

PERFORMANCE CRITICISM

Students will improve their singing ability by listening to other singers and offering constructive criticism to them.

Procedure

The teacher should divide the class into two groups. As one sings, the other listens. The roles are then reversed. Each group should discuss the other's performance, listing both the good and bad things that they heard. Some areas of discussion might include enunciation, dynamics, tempo, tone quality, balance, parts, posture, cut-offs, and attacks.

Evaluation

This entire activity is a means of evaluation. The teacher may also take notes on each performance and mention anything that the students did not hear or see. Students should not offer destructive criticism, but should try to offer constructive criticism, suggestions for improvement, and compliments when they are deserved.

RECORDING EVALUATION

Students will improve their singing ability by recording a performance and evaluating this performance.

Procedure

This is a good activity to use when preparing for a program as well as in the regular routine of the class. Students should have the number "polished" before recording. When listening, they should criticize the performance and a list of areas which need improvement may be made on the chalkboard. The song could also be recorded in the early stages of development and recorded again later after it has been "polished." The two recordings should then be compared. Students (as well as the teacher) may hear mistakes that they didn't realize were being made. This activity could also be used after a performance, such as a Christmas program or a Spring Concert.

Evaluation

Students should develop a critical ear for music and performance practices by participating in this activity. It is a very effective means of evaluation because sections can be played over as students and the teacher concentrate on the performance. Some areas of discussion might include enunciation, dynamics, tempo, tone quality, balance, parts, posture, cut-offs, and attacks.

FAVORITE SONGS

Students will develop a positive attitude toward music by singing favorite songs.

Procedure

An important part of music class is the development of positive attitudes toward singing and playing instruments. This can be promoted by the use of favorite songs selected by the students. These songs may be put into a grab bag and a few minutes can be used to draw songs from the bag to sing. The teacher could take a few minutes of the music class to let students raise their hand and select favorite songs to sing, if the grab bag seems to be too much trouble. A satisfying singing experience should be the result whichever way the activity is conducted. The teacher may also let each student choose a song they don't know to be "their" song for the year. Every week the class can learn a new song. The teacher may announce "Turn to page 12. This is 'Susan's' song."

Evaluation

Attitudes are especially difficult to evaluate. The teacher can only observe students to see if they seem to enjoy music, if they participate willingly, and if they are anxious to come to the music class. A large variety of activities and an enthusiastic teacher will aid in the development of these positive attitudes.

COMMUNITY SING

Students will improve their singing ability and develop positive attitudes toward music by participating in a "community sing."

Procedure

If it is possible to schedule grades together, the teacher may hold a "community sing" (grades one, two and three together and grades four, five and six together). These may be held once or twice a month, using familiar songs that all of the students know. Although performance practices should not be completely forgotten, this is not the time to drill students. These "community sings" should be held for the enjoyment of singing together. Each grade may have one special song to perform as the other two grades listen.

Evaluation

This activity should be used to develop positive attitudes toward music as students enjoy singing familiar songs together. The teacher should not stop the children to correct mistakes but should join together with the students in the spirit of enjoyment. Songs that have been memorized may be chosen by the students or the teacher may prepare sheets with words of familiar songs.

OSTINATO ACCOMPANIMENTS

Students will improve their playing skills by accompanying songs with ostinato patterns.

Procedure

Familiar songs should be used for this activity with few chord changes. Also, pentatonic songs may be used. If pentatonic songs are used, students may create their own ostinato patterns on the bells, xylophone, marimba, or piano (any pattern will go well together). Other songs may require the teacher's aid in setting up ostinato patterns that follow the chord changes and go well with the song. A final performance of the song may be recorded, using several ostinato patterns and a few rhythm instruments. The song may be performed several times with different students playing the instruments so that more children may develop their playing skills.

Evaluation

The teacher may evaluate students as they practice their ostinato patterns individually before trying them with the song. Each pattern should be practiced separately and then all of the instruments together before trying the song with singers and accompaniment. Students and the teacher may evaluate the performance together as they listen to the recording. Areas for discussion include balance, tempo, dynamics, texture (too many or too few instruments used in the accompaniment), mistakes made during the performance, and the singers' performance (tone quality, cut-offs, entrances, consonants, vowels, and so forth).

ROUND SEARCH

Students will improve their singing skills and understanding of rounds by finding songs that can be sung in rounds and performing these songs.

Procedure

After students have had some experience in singing rounds, the teacher may explain that not all songs can be sung as rounds. The chords must stay the same for each part of the round for it to sound correct together. This may be demonstrated by singing songs as a round that do not work, so that students will hear the dissonance. The teacher may ask students to look through books at home, in the library, or in the music room to find songs that they think will work as rounds. Songs should be tried in class to determine if they will work, and all of the rounds may be printed on a sheet to be sung.

Evaluation

The teacher can evaluate students' understanding of rounds by the examples that they bring to class and by their discussion of these songs to determine if they will work as rounds. Singing skills should also be evaluated as students strengthen their ability to sing in two and/or three parts using rounds.

PARTNER SONG SEARCH

Students will improve their singing skills and understanding of partner songs by finding songs that can be used together as partner songs and performing these songs.

Procedure

Students should begin this activity by singing several partner songs, such as "Swing Low Sweet Chariot" and "Angel Band." They may then try two songs together that will not work as partner songs. A discussion should follow to determine why some songs go well together and others do not. Students may find certain similarities in partner songs, such as the songs being in the same meter, having the same number of measures, being in the same key, and having similar chord changes. If students cannot find these similarities by examining the songs, the teacher should point them out. The teacher may ask students to look in the music books in their homes, in the library, or in the music classroom to find songs that will be satisfactory as partner songs. When songs are brought in they should be tried for the class to determine if they work well together as partner songs. These songs may be printed on a hand-out sheet for students to sing in class.

Evaluation

The teacher may evaluate students' understanding of partner songs by the examples they bring to class and by their discussion of these songs as they determine if they will be satisfactory as partner songs. Each song must be learned well before attempting to sing the two songs together. It may take several attempts before students are able to carry their own part and not get confused with the other song.

READING SONG WORDS

Students will improve their ability to read music and their playing skills by reading words from the board.

Procedure

Eight students should be given different reasonator bells comprising the C scale. Each person should recognize his pitch, and know the name of the note and where it is found on the staff. The teacher should have words spelled on the staff for the students to play:

E g g   B a d   B e a d

As the teacher points to a note, the person with that bell plays the pitch. To remain involved the other students in the class may sing the name of the note. After the eight students have played several words they should give their bells to eight other students until everyone in the class has had a turn.

Evaluation

Students may be evaluated on their ability to read the music as they play the bells and sing the name of the pitch. Words that are performed incorrectly should be repeated. A student may play the right note but not in time. When this happens the example should also be repeated.

CHORD ACCOMPANIMENTS

Students will improve their playing skills and understanding of chords by accompanying a song using resonator bells to chord.

Procedure

The teacher should begin with simple songs using one or two chord changes. These songs may be charted using colored notes (red for the C chord and blue for the G chord).

Mary Had A Little Lamb

Six students should be given resonator bells for the C chord (c, e, and g) and the G chord (g, b, and d). As the teacher points to the chord, students should play their bells together for the correct chord. All three notes must be played together to form the chord. This will normally require practice. After the song has been played successfully with the instruments alone, the words should be added. These six students may give their bells to other students until everyone in the class has chorded.

Evaluation

The most difficult part of this activity will be for students to play their three bells together. This will take practice and concentration as well as coordination. It is also difficult for students to read the music from the charted song even though the colored notes will help. The teacher should not expect success at first and should be patient as the students progress. Later, the colored notes may be eliminated as the students are able to read chords from the chart using regular notation.

PLAYING WITH NUMBERS

Students will improve their reading and playing skills by playing songs on the bells or piano using numbers.

Procedure

The teacher should copy several familiar songs using the notes and numbers:

Twinkle Twinkle Little Star

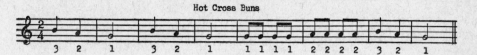

Hot Cross Buns

3 2 1 3 2 1 1 1 1 1 2 2 2 2 3 2 1

Students should go to the melody bells or the piano and play the songs. The teacher may wish to write the numbers under the notes or perhaps only the note to allow the students to figure the numbers. This may also be done with note names. Students may achieve immediate success and have a satisfying experience with numbers or note names written under the notes. They may first use notes with numbers and later advance their music reading skills by reading the music without the numbers.

Evaluation

The teacher may evaluate students as they play songs on the melody bells or piano. Some students will develop their playing skills very quickly while others will improve slowly. Students with motor and/or coordination problems will need special help and extra time for practice. The teacher may give students time to practice in class and set a special day for testing, when everyone must play a certain song. Rhythm and beat should be stressed as well as playing the correct notes.

BOTTLE PLAYING

Students will improve their concept of the scale, sound production, and playing skills by tuning pop bottles to a scale and playing songs by numbers.

Procedure

The teacher should allow students to experiment with sound production using water in pop bottles to find that the less water in the bottle the lower the sound and the more water in the bottle the higher the sound. Students may then use eight bottles to tune to a major scale by pouring different amounts of water in the bottles and blowing across the top of each bottle. These should be numbered one through eight, and songs may be played on them with charted music using numbers.

Evaluation

Evaluation should take place in three stages during this activity. First, the teacher may evaluate students as they experiment with the bottles and water. Questions should be asked to stimulate the students' thinking and lead them to the conclusion that more water in the bottles produce higher sounds and less water in the bottles produce lower sounds. This may confuse students who know that low sounds come from big musical instruments and high sounds from small musical instruments. This can be explained by looking at the air space in the bottles. The large space (with little water) produces the low sounds, and the small space (with more water) produces the high sounds. Next the students' concept of the scale may be evaluated as they tune the bottles. One student may handle the bottles and water as the remainder of the class tells him to pour more water in or out of the bottles. The teacher may find it necessary to aid students in this stage of the activity. Finally, students may be evaluated on their playing skills as they read music by the use of numbers and play the songs on the bottles. Some students may have difficulty even producing a sound on the bottles, so all students may not succeed without having had the opportunity to practice. The teacher may suggest that students try this experiment at home using their own bottles to play the songs. (Glasses filled with water and played with spoons will also be satisfactory for this activity).

TRANSPOSING SONGS

Students will improve their concept of transposition by playing and transposing songs.

Procedure

Students should have experience playing the bells, piano, marimba, or xylophone using songs with numbers. The teacher may ask students to use a different note as number one and play the song again. Students will find that the song sounds the same, only higher or lower, and the teacher can introduce the term "transposition." The teacher should use songs composed of three to six notes in the keys of C. and G for beginning experiences in transposition. Students will not need to use sharps or flats with these keys. Later, as students' concept of transposition and their playing skills improve, they may transpose using other keys.

Evaluation

The teacher may evaluate students' understanding of transposition as they explain what happened when they used a different note as number one while playing the songs. If students cannot verbalize the experience, the teacher may give an explanation as the word "transposition" is introduced. Further evaluation can be made as students transpose many songs in different keys.

PLAYING THE RECORDER

Students will improve their playing skills by playing songs on a recorder.

Procedure

Sometime during the third or fourth grade students should be involved in a unit using recorders. Many method books are available for teaching the recorder. The teacher should choose one that will meet the needs of the class. This may be a concentrated unit teaching only the recorder. Recorders can also be used with regular songs used in the class playing simple phrases and portions of the songs. After an introduction to the recorder, students should continue to use the instrument throughout the sixth grade to develop their playing skills and to add pleasing accompaniments to songs sung in class.

Evaluation

Evaluation is an important aspect of teaching a unit on recorders. When the teacher assigns a lesson and has students play together many students will depend on a few leaders following their fingering and hiding behind the sound of many recorders. The teacher should take time to listen to the students individually or to small groups of students as they play short phrases of a song. This will take a considerable amount of time, but the final results will be much better. If three people play an assigned phrase together the teacher can watch fingerings, posture, breathing, and listen to the tone quality and it will not take as long to hear the entire class. Students may be arranged in seats or chairs (first, second, third, and so forth) or assigned grades after their playing test.

PLAYING THE AUTOHARP

Students will develop their playing skills by playing the autoharp.

Procedure

Students may begin playing the autoharp by using one person to strum and several students to push different chord buttons as the teacher points to the people to change the chords. Next, one person strums and one person pushes all of the chord buttons reading where the chord changes occur himself. Finally, one person should be able to strum, change chords, and read the music alone.

Evaluation

The teacher must evaluate students to determine when they are ready to advance from one method of playing the autoharp to another. This will take practice, so a center could be set up outside of the music room where the students could go to play songs on the autoharp. Since this is an instrument used primarily for accompaniment, the students should be encouraged to sing as they play the autoharp.

PLAYING DUETS

Students will improve their playing skills by playing duets.

Procedure

After students have developed skill in playing instruments (such as the piano, bells, marimba, autoharp, or recorder) the teacher may assign duets. Any combination of instruments could be used and even trios or quartets could be arranged. The teacher will need to arrange music for these various ensembles:

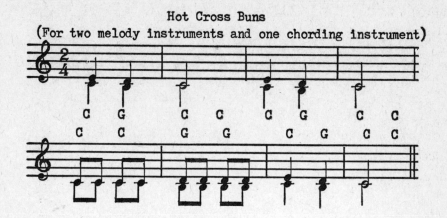

Hot Cross Buns
(For two melody instruments and one chording instrument)

Evaluation

The teacher may let students form their own duets, trios, or quartets and allow time during the class period for practice. A day may be set aside for a concern during which everyone will play for the class. Rules regarding etiquette for attendance at a concert can be developed before students listen to the ensembles. Evaluation should be made by the teacher as the students perform during the concert.

CHORDING ON THE PIANO

Students will improve their concept of chords and playing skills by playing chords on the piano.

Procedure

The teacher may assign three students to play different chords on the piano (two-note or three-note chords in any inversion). Any familiar song using three chord changes may be used. As the students sing the teacher should point to the people playing the chords to indicate to 'them when to change chords. The chords could also be charted and the teacher point to the correct chord on the chart. Another variation would be to let students choose the chord they think goes best with the melody. This will develop ear training, harmony, and playing skills.

Evaluation

If students choose the chord changes themselves, this should be done at the beginning of the activity and listed on the board. They may sing the song (as the teacher chords) and raise their hand when they think the chord changes. After the changes are identified and listed on the board, students may be chosen to play the chords on the piano. The teacher may evaluate playing skills at this time.

Chapter 8

Theory, Terms, Composers and Games

Activities in this section will deal with methods and techniques designed to improve the students' knowledge of music theory, terms, and composers. Note placement on the staff will be presented through games and work sheets. Forms will be introduced beginning with simple binary and ternary forms and progressing to more complicated forms, such as the fugue and sonata allegro forms. Word puzzles and term activities will further the students' knowledge of musical symbols, terms and elements. Major and minor scales will also be introduced by use of whole and half step systems for their construction. Music history and composers will be dealt with as students complete the activities presented.

NOTE TICKETS

Students will improve their understanding of note placement on the staff by standing in the correct position on a large floor staff.

Procedure

The teacher should prepare a large floor staff (showing the treble and bass clefs) and two inch by four inch tickets showing notes on the staff:

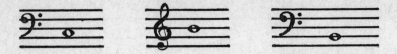

These tickets are distributed to the class. Each student must find his place on the staff. After students are standing (or sitting) on the correct line or space the teacher may pass out new tickets. This activity can also be used as a relay with two teams. The winning team may choose a pop record to hear or a favorite activity to do.

Evaluation

Students may be evaluated by their ability to place themselves on the correct line or space of the staff. Later, students may be given tickets with only a letter (such as E, B, or G) and find their places on the staff. If the activity is used as a relay, two team members may go to the staff at one time and the person who gets in the proper position first wins the point for his team.

NOTE TOSS

Students will improve their understanding of note placement on the staff by playing a note toss game.

Procedure

A large staff must be constructed on the floor using masking tape which indicates each line and space receiving a certain number of points:

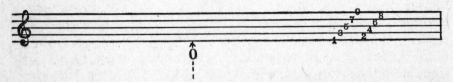

Using a one pound coffee can lid, students line up and slide the lid on the floor trying to place it on the staff. Once the lid has landed on a line or space students must name the note to receive the points. Students can keep track of their own points, and the one with the most points when time is called wins the game.

Evaluation

Students may be evaluated on their ability to name notes after they have placed the lid on a line or space. This activity may be used as a motivational technique when the teacher has tried work sheets and theory papers and students still do not know note names. Students will enjoy the game and want to know how to figure the note names to win points.

PLAYING BY SKIPS AND STEPS

Students will improve their concept of melodic notation by using a step figure and transferring this to a keyboard.

Procedure

Several figures should be available showing ascending and descending passages by steps and skips:

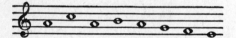 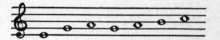

Students should then read the notes from these figures and play them on a keyboard instrument. Other figures may be added using simple melodic examples moving in steps or skips.

Evaluation

The teacher may evaluate students by their ability to play the figures on a keyboard instrument. If students are not able to play the figure they may be asked to stop and verbalize the melodic movement (for example, "It goes up three notes by skip, down four notes by step, and up three notes by step). After noting the movement they should be able to play it correctly.

GRAND STAFF PLACEMENT

Students will improve their concept of melodic movement and placement on the staff by moving on a large staff.

Procedure

The teacher should prepare a large floor staff of masking tape and cards with directions to the students (such as, start on the second line, move up four by steps, move down two by skip, move up one by skip, stay the same for two beats). This activity may be used as a relay game with two teams. Each "direction" card is different. One member of opposing teams comes forward, takes a direction card and follows the directions. If the student performs the moves correctly he wins a point for his team and the next team member is given a card. (Moving for the example above he starts on G, moves up, stepping on each line and space (four) to D, moves down two by skip to G, again stepping only on the lines, and stays on G for two beats hopping two times). Everyone on each team acts out the directions on a card and the team with the most points wins the game.

Evaluation

Students' understanding of melodic movement by step, skip, or staying the same may be evaluated by their ability to move on the staff correctly. The teacher should observe closely, and if many students are having difficulty, other activities involving melodic movement should be utilized. If most of the students are doing well, the teacher may make the "direction" cards more difficult and give easier "direction" cards to the slow learners.

LINES AND SPACES

Students will improve their understanding of note placement on the staff by identifying line and space notes.

Procedure

The teacher should prepare Figures A, B, C, and D on the chalkboard and on flashcards containing notes:

FLASHCARDS

The teacher may refer to Figure A as notes placed on spaces are explained and to Figure B as notes placed on lines are explained. Next, Figures C and D should be discussed as the students tell which notes are on lines and which notes are on spaces. Finally, the teacher may hold up flash cards as students say "line" or "space." After the class has worked together in this manner (identifying line and space notes) a work sheet may be prepared.

Evaluation

After explaining note placement on lines or spaces of the staff, the teacher may evaluate the students' understanding if they are able to verbalize correctly. When the work sheets are collected the teacher can make a more accurate evaluation of each students' understanding of the concept.

MUSICAL NOTE NAME GAME

Students will improve their understanding of note names by raising a card as the teacher calls out a letter name.

Procedure

Cards containing a staff with a note placed on it are placed in a circle on the floor. As music is played, students walk around in a circle and when the music stops each student stops behind a card. As the teacher calls a letter every student with that note on it raises his card. The music begins again and a different letter is called when the music stops. (For variety each student could raise his note and tell it's name quickly when the music stops.)

Evaluation

The teacher may evaluate students as they raise their card when a note is called. Students may be asked if they see other (E's) on the floor before starting the music again. If students are going around the circle and naming each note they may be evaluated as they call out the letter. If they are wrong another student may help them find the proper letter. If they are correct the next person announces the name of his note.

WORK SHEET NOTES

Students will improve their understanding of note placement and melodic movement by answering questions on a work sheet.

Procedure

The teacher should prepare a work sheet using directions to reinforce concepts of note placement and melodic movement. Only a few examples have been presented here but similar questions can be made up to fill the entire sheet. (Blank staffs should be provided).

1. Make five notes going up.

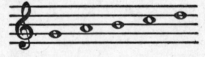

2. Make six notes going down.

3. Make two notes going up by step and one going down by skip.

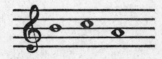

4. Make two notes staying the same, four going up by step and two going down by skip.

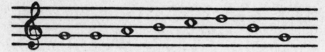

5. Color the notes in the spaces red.

6. Color the notes on the lines blue.

Evaluation

The teacher may evaluate students as their papers are handed in and checked. Usually, most of the students will be able to succeed but, for the slow learners, the teacher may allow students who finish quickly to help them. This is a good technique to use in most written work. It gives students who are finished something constructive to do and should be a helpful activity for all concerned.

NOTE RELAY GAME

Students will improve their concept of note placement on the staff by playing a note relay game.

Procedure

Students should have had experiences notating letters on the staff before attempting this activity. Two staffs should be placed on the chalkboard and the class divided into two teams. The teacher displays a word as a member from each team notates it on the staff. The one who is finished first wins the point for his team.

The next member of each team comes forward and the game continues. Some words that could be used include:

fag	egg	feed	begged
add	cafe	faced	bee
face	adage	gag	ade
bagged	ace	bag	gage
dab	ebb	beef	beaded
baa	cage	decade	bad
fade	cabbage	age	babe
baggage	beg	deed	added
fad	bed	bead	gagged
dad	edge	faded	Ed

Evaluation

The teacher may evaluate students as they notate words at the chalkboard. If students are not successful, the teacher may need to review note placement on the staff. If students are slow, additional practice at this game should improve their speed and ability. An activity such as this should be used for reinforcement and motivation and should move quickly in order to keep the excitement going.

WRITTEN WORK SHEET

Students will improve their concept of note names and placement on the staff by filling out a work sheet.

Procedure

The teacher should prepare a work sheet using material similar to the following:

1. Draw these notes on the proper line or space of the staff.

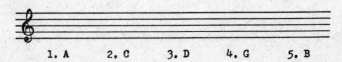

1. A   2. C   3. D   4. G   5. B

2. Name these notes.

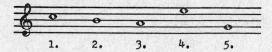

3. Name these notes that use ledger lines.

4. Draw these notes two different places on the staff.

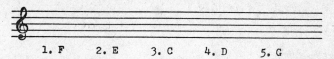

1. F   2. E   3. C   4. D   5. G

5. Read the following story by naming the notes on the staff.

went to the store to get an

and • A

chased him past the   and

he ran into the store just in time. The store keeper

up the bill but   had lost his money. He had to go home

and get some more money from his

Evaluation

The teacher may evaluate students by collecting the papers and checking their answers. At first, work sheets may be given as homework or classwork where students can help each other. The teacher may check both of these but the most accurate evaluation will be a work sheet used as a test to evaluate the individuals' learnings and understandings.

FORM SHAPES

Students will improve their understanding of form by using colored shapes to represent phrases or sections.

Procedure

This activity may be used to show form in songs that the students are singing or hearing. First, the song (or listening example) should be divided into phrases or sections. Students are then given colored shapes to represent the form of the song, such as the following:

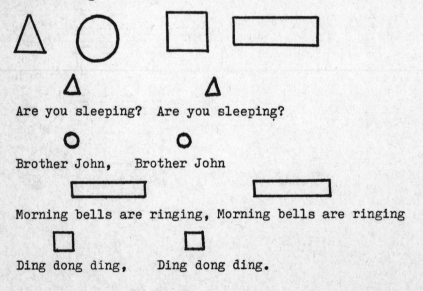

If a phrase or section is the same, "like" shapes should be used and a different shape used if it is not the same. "Are You Sleeping" has been divided into short phrases with the proper shape listed above. Other examples may not use such short phrases, but the procedure for identifying them will be the same.

Evaluation

The teacher may evaluate students as they come to the front of the class and arrange the colored shapes in order. If they are not correct, the students at their seats may help make corrections. In this example eight students could have been given a shape and arranged themselves in order holding up their shapes to show the form of the song or listening example. This activity may be advanced as students give letter names to phrases or sections instead of using shapes.

FORM ACTIONS

Students will improve their concept of form by using different actions for phrases or sections.

Procedure

This activity may be used with a song that students are singing or with a listening example. Before attempting the lesson, students should have had experience dividing the music into sections or phrases. After the music has been divided into sections or phrases the teacher should let students suggest actions for each part. If phrases are alike, the same action should be performed. If they are different, unlike actions should be performed. The teacher should encourage students to be creative in their selections of actions using new combinations for variety. After actions are assigned, the song should be sung or the listening example played another time as students perform the actions to show the form.

A—Walk
B—Turn
C—Knee Bends
A—Walk

Evaluation

The teacher may evaluate students' understanding of phrasing and sections as they begin the activity by dividing the song. Because some songs can be divided into phrases or sections in different ways, the teacher may need to suggest the most appropriate way if and when students cannot decide. Students may then be evaluated on their creative ability as they suggest actions for the phrases. Finally, their understanding of form can be evaluated as they decide if phrases are alike or different and as they assign letter names and perform the actions. The teacher may find that some students lack coordination when performing the actions to the music. Notes can be made if this is the case and additional activities used to strengthen students' coordination.

FORM REPORTS

Students will improve their understanding of form by giving reports on various kinds of forms used in music.

Procedure

The teacher may assign reports to various students on the following forms:

1. Two part (Binary)

2. Three part (Ternary)

3. Rondo

4. Variation

5. Sonata Allegro (Expanded ABA, two themes—development—restatement)

6. Suite (Dance suites of the sixteenth and seventeenth centuries—Allemande, Courante, Saraband, and Gigue).

7. Tone poem (Form dictated by a story or description of a character)

8. Opera, Oratorio, Cantata (Large vocal works, recitative—aria)

9. Fugue (Complex polyphonic form—one theme introduced by two or more voices in turn, developed in what can be considered another section, then restated in the final part of the form)

After students report on their assigned form, examples should be studied in class using songs or listening examples. Students may try composing their own songs using some of the more simple forms.

Evaluation

The teacher may evaluate students as they give their reports on an assigned form. It may be necessary to explain the report and interpret parts that the students do not understand. This can be accomplished further by presenting examples of music in the form being studied. Evaluation can be made as students apply the information in the report to the example of music selected by the teacher. Each example should be heard or sung several times in order for the students to apply their knowledge of form to the music.

RHYTHM RONDO

Students will improve their understanding of the rondo form by creating and performing a rhythm rondo.

Procedure

The teacher should write a two measure rhythmic example on the chalkboard to represent the section A of the rondo:

Every time the A theme returns the class should clap this together. Individual students are chosen to represent the B, C, and D sections. When it is their turn they improvise a rhythmic pattern in order for the composition to develop as follows:

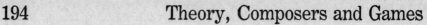

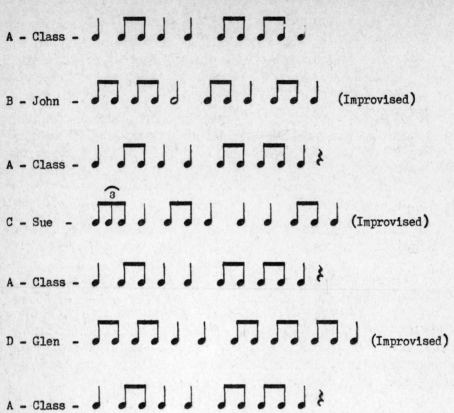

The composition could have first been written on the board and different sections assigned to different rhythm instruments to play as the students read the music from the chalkboard.

Evaluation

The teacher may evaluate students' understanding of the rondo form as they create the rhythmic composition. If improvising (as in the first example), students must be sure to use the entire eight counts. If reading the rhythms from the board, the teacher should go over each section individually until the group can play their part. Identification of the rondo form in a listening example can be used as a further means of evaluation.

SONGS IN FORM

Students will improve their understanding of form by singing different songs in a special order to demonstrate form.

Procedure

Students should be divided into three or four groups naming each group B, C, or D. (Group A will be everyone singing together on "Twinkle Twinkle Little Star.") Each group chooses a song on a certain subject or just a favorite song. Groups sing their songs to demonstrate certain forms.

> A—"Twinkle Twinkle Little Star"
> B—"Johnny Works"
> A—"Twinkle Twinkle Little Star"

A—"Twinkle Twinkle Little Star"
B—"Johnny Works"
C—"Where is the Penny?"
A—"Twinkle Twinkle Little Star"

A—"Twinkle Twinkle Little Star"
B—"Johnny Works"
A—"Twinkle Twinkle Little Star"
C—"Where is the Penny?"
A—"Twinkle Twinkle Little Star"
D—"Paw Paw Patch"
A—"Twinkle Twinkle Little Star"

Evaluation

The teacher should list each form to be sung on the chalkboard (ABA, ABCA, ABACADA). Students may be evaluated as they sing songs in the correct form. If there is confusion the teacher should make certain that students know which group they are in (B, C, or D and everyone on A). The concept of form may be further evaluated after the students listen to (or sing) songs and identify the form.

CREATING SONGS IN FORM

Students will strengthen their creative ability and their understanding of form by creating a song using ABA, ABACA and ABCA form.

Procedure

Three students should be selected to create a phrase on the bells or rhythm instrument. The first student comes forward and creates his phrase to be named the "A" phrase. The student must be able to play the phrase again without mistakes, so it should not be long or complicated. The next student comes forward and creates his phrase to be named "B," and then phrase "C" is created by the third student. The teacher then writes the three forms on the chalkboard (ABA, ABCA, and ABACA). Each student plays his phrase in the proper order to create songs in various forms. These students should choose three other students to take their place for the purpose of creating new melodies as the activity continues.

Evaluation

Students may be evaluated on their ability to create melodies as they play the bells to create a phrase. The teacher may need to caution them to make the melody simple so that they can repeat it several times. Each student must practice until this can be accomplished. Students may also be evaluated on their playing skills as well as on their ability to memorize a passage. Some students will find these things very easy while others may not be able to succeed. The teacher may offer suggestions for students who cannot think of a phrase or simplify a phrase for a student who does not have coordination enough to play a more difficult phrase. Students then may be evaluated on their understanding of form as they play at the proper times to create a song in the form written on the chalkboard.

VARIATION OF A THEME

Students will improve their understanding of Theme and Variations by listening to a recording using this form and discussing ways in which the composition was varied.

Procedure

This activity should begin with a discussion of the word "vary." ("What does it mean to vary something?") Students should come to the conclusion that when something is varied it is changed. They may then apply this to a recording of a theme and variations. Students should be familiar with the theme of the recording before it is played by singing or playing the theme on the piano. After the recording is played, a list may be made of ways that this music (or any theme) may be varied. Students may further the activity by taking a simple theme, such as the first phrase of "Twinkle

Twinkle Little Star," and writing their own variations. The list of ways to vary music might include the following:

1. Change of timbre (instruments)
2. Change of register (octave)
3. Change of meter
4. Change of mode or key
5. Change of tempo
6. Change of dynamics
7. Alteration of tones in melody
8. Alteration of rhythmic patterns
9. Use of imitation
10. Use of retrograde
11. Use of inversion
12. Addition of sharps or flats to alter tones
13. Addition of notes
14. Change of texture

Evaluation

The teacher may evaluate students' understanding of Variations by their discussion of the ways in which the music was varied. If students cannot express how the music was changed the teacher may find it necesary to tell them (after listening to the first recording) and test their learning as they listen to and discuss different recordings. Only the most obvious changes should be noted for each recording, so the complete list of variations may never occur in any one song.

WRITING A VARIATION

Students will further their creative ability and understanding of musical form by writing a variation on a theme.

Procedure

Each student should be given a paper with a simple theme (such as, "Twinkle Twinkle Little Star") and several blank staffs below it. Any theme may be used as long as it is simple and familiar to the students. A discussion should be held listing ways that a

theme can be varied. (Refer to the previous activity.) The teacher
may want to spend several class meetings discussing, hearing and
studying variations before the class attempts to write variations.
At the onset, students should choose only two ways to vary the
theme. Later, as they advance, they may vary the theme using
many (or all) of the methods listed in the previous activity.

VARIATION CHANGING RHYTHMS AND
ADDING SHARPS OR FLATS

ORIGINAL

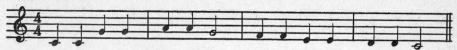

VARIATION

Evaluation

The teacher may evaluate students by collecting their papers
and checking their work. Even though variations have been made,
rhythms, notes, sharps, and flats should be used correctly. Students enjoy hearing their variations and all should be played if
possible. If this is not possible, a few of the better variations may
be played.

SCRAMBLED FORM

Students will improve their listening skills and concept of form
by listening to a record and listing a scrambled form in the proper
order.

Procedure

The teacher should prepare a worksheet for a listening example, listing everything that happens in the music in a scrambled
order. Each worksheet will differ according to the listening exam-

ple. The teacher may use the following guide (prepared to use with a pop record):

"A	Verse 1
B	Chorus 4 (No drums at end)
C	Interlude
D	Chrous 1 (With drums at end)
E	Chorus 6 (Fade out)
F	Introduction
G	Verse 2
H	Chorus 2 (With drums at end)
I	Chorus 3 (With drums at end)
J	Chorus 5 (With drums at end)"[11]

Evaluation

The teacher may evaluate the students' work by collecting and grading their papers. Students should be familiar with the terms included on the work sheet before attempting this activity (verse, chorus, interlude, coda, introduction). If students do poorly on this activity, the terms should be reviewed and the listening examples discussed in class. The listening examples may also need to be shortened and simplified until students can succeed. Gradually the teacher can advance to more difficult materials.

SINGING CONVERSATION

Students will strengthen their creative ability, gain a better understanding of opera, and strengthen their ability to match tones by singing a conversation.

Procedure

The teacher should explain to the class how to sing a conversation (the instructions may even be sung to the class). Melodies may

---

[11]Michael Don Bennett, *Surviving in General Music.* (881 S. Cooper, Memphis, Tennessee, Pop Hits Publishing, 1974) p.3.

be improvised when using this material for a creative activity. Choose a simple pattern and fit the conversation to the pattern if this material is used for matching tones. Simple melodic patterns should be used:

A conversation might proceed as follows:

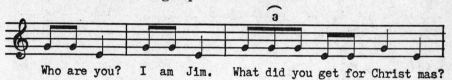

Evaluation

The teacher may evaluate students by listening as they improvise conversations. These conversations should be spontaneous. It may require several attempts at this type of activity before students are able to carry on spontaneous conversations without inhibition. Starting at an early age with this kind of activity will help a great deal. If using a specific melodic pattern, the teacher may listen to hear if students are able to continue with the correct pattern (offering assistance when it is needed). It might be helpful if the beginning remarks of each class were made in a singing conversation.

WRITING OPERAS AND MUSICALS

Students will increase their understanding of opera and musicals by writing a play and adding songs to it.

Procedure

Because music classes are limited in time, students may write the play at home. The best play may be selected, or a committee could be chosen to write the play. Once the play has been selected, the students should compose songs to be used with it. Students may set some of the speaking parts of the play to music and compose other songs at various time intervals. They may use familiar melodies and write new verses in order to save time. Familiar songs could be used with original words if they fit the theme of the play. The "musical" or "opera" could then be performed for another class, the PTA, or as a special program.

Evaluation

Although a good performance is desirable, this is not the most important result from this activity. The actual learnings gained from the development of the "musical" or "opera" are most beneficial to the student. Students should learn to cooperate, share in the responsibility, become more at ease in performing, gain an understanding of what a musical and opera are, and share in the excitement of creating a large production.

MYSTERY WORD

Students will become aware of various musical terms by guessing a mystery word for the day.

Procedure

The teacher should tell children at the beginning of class that a mystery word will be used. This word will be used three times, normally without calling attention to it. At the end of the class period students try to guess the mystery word.

Evaluation

This mystery word may be a familiar term to be reviewed or a new term to be introduced. Students should also be asked the meaning of the word after it has been discovered. This activity will keep students alert, motivate them to listen closely, and expand their musical vocabulary.

SUPPLY THE MYSTERY WORD

Students will improve their understanding of various musical terms by filling in a mystery word.

Procedure

The teacher should prepare a work sheet using various musical terms that students have studied and used. These words should be represented by a blank for the students to complete. Using the following questions as an example, the teacher can make enough questions to fill the entire work sheet:

1. A whole _____.

2. A_____ has five lines and four spaces.

3. Less than a half note, but greater than an eighth note _____.

4. Drums belong to the _____ family.

5. Violin, viola, bass violin _____.

6. A guitar belongs to the _____ family.

7. Less than a whole note, but greater than a quarter note _____.

8. A melody may be also called a _____.

9. Woodwind, string, percussion, and _____.

10. A word for "gradually get softer" _____.

11. A conductor uses this _____.

12. A keyboard instrument with pipes _____.

13. They perform at half time _____.

14. A composer who lost his hearing _____.

15. A famous child composer _____.

Evaluation

Students may be evaluated on their ability to fill in the blanks with the correct word. Written assignments such as this should always be returned to the students as soon as possible and discussed in detail. The discussion of corrected papers should be a significant learning experience.

MUSICAL PUZZLES

Students will improve their recognition and understanding of musical terms by completing word puzzles.

Procedure

The teacher may use puzzles found in various resource materials or develop word puzzles to be used in class. The following may be used as examples for the purpose of creating new puzzles:

PERCUSSION PUZZLE

```
C Y M B A L A N S
E A C E B A E C N
L D E L O F M L A
E F O L G C B A R
S O P S O K T V E
T R I A N G L E D
O B A B G A O S R
K O N A B O M A U
B A O R P D R U M
```

Snare Drum	Cymbal	Bells
Celeste	Claves	Triangle
Piano	Drum	Gong

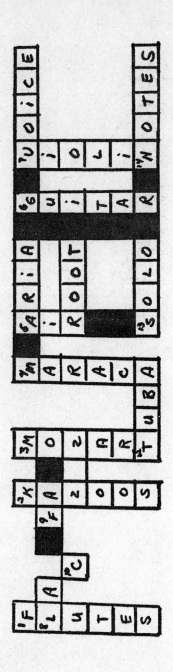

Across

5. Vocal solo in opera
7. Human instrument
8. Sixth tone of the scale
9. Fourth tone of the scale
10. Middle _____
11. Bottom note of a chord
12. Lowest brass instrument
13. One performer
14. Written on the staff (plural)

Down

1. Silver or wooden instrument (plural)
2. Hum into it (plural)
3. The wonder child
4. Latin American Gourd
5. Old word for melody
6. Stringed instrument (six strings)
7. Stringed instrument (four strings)

INSTRUMENT PUZZLE

QUESTIONS TO INSTRUMENT PUZZLE

ACROSS

1, A family of instruments

3. A percussion instrument that rings

4. Woodwind that looks like a clarinet

6. A stringed instrument placed between the knees

7. A brass instrument with bright tone

9. Highest stringed instrument

10. Family of instruments

12. High woodwind

13. Percussion instrument you shake to play

DOWN

1. One instrument playing

2. A folk stringed instrument

3. A low woodwind

5. A small group playing

7. A brass instrument with a slide

8. A low brass instrument

11. Woodwind that can play very high or low

HIDDEN WORD PUZZLE

```
C L A R I N E T B R A S S
E O B A C O T R E E R O T
L A F L A T B D L S I N A
L E F D B E P M L T A G F
O B O E C O R B A S S O F
T D R U M B C O C O U N T
I O M P D R A N B L U E S
E P I A N O C E R O C K E
```

Blues	Oboe	Cello	Piano	Brass
Trombone	Bass	Aria	Rest	Form
Tie	Staff	Rock	Song	Drum
Note	Clarinet	Flat	Solo	

Evaluation

The teacher may collect the papers and grade the puzzles or read the answers in class in order that students can grade their own work. At some time the correct answers should be given, even if the teacher has corrected the papers using check marks for wrong answers. This will reinforce the correct answer for students and result in a learning experience.

SONG PUZZLE

Students will improve their knowledge of the use of musical symbols by constructing a puzzle.

Procedure

The teacher should prepare packets with a card containing three to five measures. The packet also contains nine to fifteen small cards. These small cards have parts of the complete staff. Students should place the small cards under the large card reconstructing the measures:

LARGE CARD

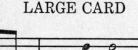

SMALL CARDS

Evaluation

This activity is good to use in learning centers because students can evaluate themselves when the small cards are put together to match the large card. The teacher may walk around the room and give help to any students having difficulty. When students have completed a packet they may put all the cards back in the packet and trade with someone else who has also completed the work.

MUSICAL RIDDLES

Students will improve their knowledge of musical terms by guessing the answers to riddles.

Procedure

A riddle should be written on the chalkboard on Monday with several lines drawn under it. Through the week students may come in and write their answers on the lines. On Friday, the winner is announced (the first person who puts the correct answer). Students should write their names beside their answer so the teacher can tell who is the winner.

I have a head and it is black.   (Sixteenth note)
I carry a stem upon my back   _____
Two flags I take along with me,   _____
Now what do you think I could be?   _____

Five big lines and four spaces   (Staff)
Where musical notes put their faces   _____
          _____
          _____

I am graceful and I swirl   (Ballerina)
I dance on my toes as I twirl.   _____
          _____
          _____

Not once but twice is my game.   (Repeat sign)
Two dots remind you of my name.   _____
          _____
          _____

Listen to the band with your ear.   (Piccolo)
I'm the highest sound that you hear.   _____
          _____
          _____

Evaluation

This is an activity that should be used for fun and to motivate students. The teacher should not tell the correct answer until Friday so that students keep on guessing through the week. There will probably be no follow-up on this activity even if the riddle is not answered correctly. A new riddle can be placed on the chalkboard for the next week. At first, students may be enthusiastic about the game and later lose some of their enthusiasm. When this happens new motivational activities should be found and put to use.

MAJOR AND MINOR SCALE CONSTRUCTION

Students will improve their understanding of scales by using a formula of whole and half steps to form a major or minor scale.

Procedure

The teacher may explain a scale as being eight sequential notes beginning and ending on the same note (remembering that in music when you get to G, start over on A). Let students write scales according to this formula. (Also write them on the staff).

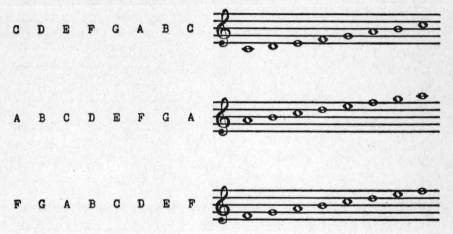

The teacher should play the scales and students will find that they are not all major scales. (They will know that they do not sound right, but they won't know why). The teacher may explain that there has to be a certain combination of whole and half steps to create a major scale. Have a large keyboard where all of the students can see it. Check the C Scale to find that formula.

As students observe the large keyboard they should check each note of the other scales to see which notes need to be sharped or flatted in order to form the correct combination of whole and half steps to create a major scale. Write each scale on the staff.

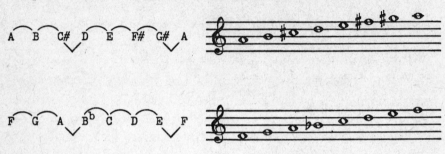

Evaluation

To do this activity students must know what a half step and what a whole step are and that a sharp raises a note and a flat lowers it. The teacher may evaluate students' knowledge of scales by their ability to construct a major scale beginning on any note. After students can construct major scales they may try natural (or pure) minor scales.

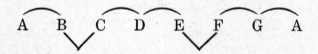

DYNAMIC CHARACTERS

Students will improve their understanding of dynamic shadings and tempo markings by associating them with animals or characters.

Procedure

The teacher may make colorful charts to display in various parts of the room, using animals to represent dynamic shadings and tempo markings. Some associations used might be as follows:

1. Soft—p—Butterfly

2. Medium loud—mf—Dog

3. Loud—f—Elephant

4. Adagio—Turtle

5. Presto—Road Runner

Evaluation

The teacher may evaluate the success of these charts by students' ability to recognize tempo and dynamic markings. They should be more aware of their presence in music and use them when singing songs and playing musical instruments. The teacher could also ask students to draw animals to associate with musical terms. The best of these could be displayed about the room.

MOOD COMPOSITIONS

Students will improve their concept of mood by composing two compositions that contrast in mood.

Procedure

The class should be divided into groups of from four to six students. Each group should be asked to compose two pieces that have different moods (happy—sad, excited—sorrowful, calm—lively). They may use body sounds, rhythm instruments, or sounds on their desks to develop the composition. After students have worked in their groups for ten minutes, they should perform for each other.

Evaluation

The teacher should evaluate the students' work by the discussion that follows the performance of their compositions. Some questions that might be asked include the following:

1. How were the two feelings achieved?
2. How did the sound differ when the mood was changed?
3. How would you change the composition?

MOOD ACCOMPANIMENTS

Students will increase their understanding of mood and improve their creative ability by creating an accompaniment to two poems contrasting in mood.

Procedure

Read two poems of contrasting mood to the class. Discuss the mood of the poems and what musical instrument would best fit the mood of the poems. Have several students recite the poem with an improvised rhythmic accompaniment. Do the same for the second poem and then discuss the difference in mood, the selection of the instruments, and the type of rhythmic accompaniment that was used to portray the two moods.

Evaluation

Much of the evaluation comes from the discussion before the performance. Students should be encouraged to list several words of emotion to describe the two poems (quiet, lazy, sad, choppy, harsh, exciting). The teacher may also evaluate students during their performance. They should be encouraged to speak clearly and with expression when reciting the poem. Students lacking in coordination and playing skills should be noted as well as those who are hesitant to improvise an accompaniment. Additional activities may be used for these students.

DYNAMIC CREATIONS

Students will improve their concept of dynamics by creating a composition using dynamics.

Procedure

The teacher should divide the students into groups of four to six students after they have discussed the use of loudness and softness in music. Students should then go to their groups and plan a composition using single sounds, combinations of sounds, and different dynamic levels. They may use rhythm instruments, body sounds, or sounds at their desks to create the composition. After ten minutes, the students should meet together again and play their compositions for each other.

Evaluation

The teacher may evaluate students by discussing their compositions. Attention should be focused on what degree of loudness or softness was used most frequently. The teacher may wish to introduce such terms as *forte, piano,* or *mezzo forte* at the end of the discussion. Further studies may include listening to records and discussing the use of dynamics.

SOFT AND LOUD CHARTS

Students will improve their concept of dynamics by holding up and responding to "soft" and "loud" charts.

Procedure

The teacher should prepare two large charts, one with the letter "p" and one with the letter "f." As students sing a familiar song, a leader comes to the front of the room and holds the "p" and "f" charts. When he wants the class to sing loud he holds up the "f" chart and the "p" chart whenever he wants the students to sing softly. He may change whenever he wants and the students must respond to whichever chart is displayed.

Evaluation

The teacher may evaluate students by their response to the "p" and "f" charts. The leader should be cautioned to not change so fast that the students do not have time to change their dynamic level. Later, other charts may be added with additional dynamic levels (such as, pp, mp, mf, ff).

INFORMATION HUNT

Students will improve their knowledge of music by going on an "information hunt."

TIME LINE

Procedure

The teacher should put the names of two composers on a blank bulletin board. This may be a contest between two teams in a class or between two classes. The team members are to write reports, collect articles, cut out pictures or draw pictures about their composer. The team with the most information at the end of two weeks is the winner. The composers chosen should be as equally famous as possible so each team will have an equal chance to find information. Some good choices are Bach, Beethoven, Mozart, Chopin, Haydn, etc.

Evaluation

The teacher may review information on the board with the students. Individuals could summarize their information. After all the information on both sides has been reviewed a written test could be given.

MUSICAL TIME LINE

Students will improve their knowledge of musical events by using a "Time Line."

Procedure

For students to gain a concept of historical and musical events the teacher may prepare a "Time Line." This time line may be posted in the room and referred to when singing or listening to music of a certain period.

TIME LINE (cont.)[12]

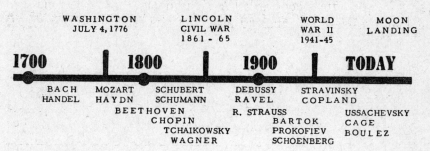

Evaluation

The teacher could require students to memorize the time line and give a test on it, but it would probably be sufficient to display the time line in the room as a reference. The teacher may assign different dates (1400, 1800, 1900) and ask students to find other events that were happening. Use of a time line as a reference will give students a total view of what has happened in music from the Gregorian Chant to the present forms.

CLUE STORY

Students will improve their knowledge about composers by listening to clues, guessing the name of the composer, and listening to a story about the composer.

Procedure

The teacher should read several clues to the class until they have guessed the name of the composer. The clues for Mozart might include some of the following:

1. He wrote operas.
2. He died a pauper.
3. He spent money foolishly.
4. He was composing at age six.
5. He and his sister went on concert tours when they were children.
6. He wrote *The Marriage of Figgaro*.

[12]From the book, *Music Handbook for the Elementary School* by Marvin Greenberg and Beatrix MacGregor, © 1972 by Parker Publishing Company, Inc. Published by Parker Publishing Company, Inc., West Nyack, New York 10994.

As the teacher reads each clue the students try to guess the composer. The clues begin by being general, then get more specific. When the composer has been guessed, the teacher should tell the entire story of the composer.

Evaluation

The teacher may determine students' knowledge of composers by seeing how many clues it takes for them to guess the name of the composer. If they are unable to guess it she may proceed with the story and give the same clues another day. A written test may be given after several clue stories have been told.

INFORMATION RACE

Students will improve their knowledge of music by racing to find information on a certain subject.

Procedure

The teacher should divide the class into four or five groups with each group having the same resource book and a list of identical questions. These questions may be about music, composers, instruments, notation, elements, including times, dates, etc. When the signal "Go!" is given each group begins searching for the information. The group to finish first is the winner.

Evaluation

The class should check the group that is the "winner." As each question is answered there may be discussion or additional information given. At the end of several of these sessions an oral review or a written examination may be given.

COMPOSER CARD GAME

Students will extend their knowledge of composers by playing a card game.

Procedure

The teacher should prepare two sets of cards, one containing three facts about a composer and one containing the composer's name. Each player receives five cards. The remaining cards are stacked in the center of the table. When it is a player's turn he must draw one card from the center stack. If he can match a composer card with a fact card he lays these two cards down, face up. When the center stack is gone the game ends and the person with the most sets is the winner.

Evaluation

This activity should increase the students' knowledge about various composers, the music they wrote, and facts about their lives. The teacher may evaluate this knowledge by giving a written examination after the students have played with the cards several times.

Chapter 9

Individualized
Music Activities

MUSIC LEARNING CENTERS

A modern and complete elementary music program should include many opportunities for reinforcement of concepts as well as a wide variety of activities. These goals can be accomplished by setting up learning centers.

The following learning centers have been set up for the average size room with twenty-five students. Each center should accommodate five people; however, more people could go to centers or fewer centers could be used with more students on each center. Teachers can adjust the number of centers and students according to her (his) room size.

The noise factor plays a big part in setting up the centers. Usually one "loud" activity should be set up in the hall and one in the room with three other quiet activities. Activities should require approximately the same amount of time, so that a time limit can be set and all groups change on signal. In this manner each group can get to all learning centers. If five minutes is spent at each center, all centers can be visited during one class period. The teacher may wish to set longer time limits or let students choose centers and stay or move about the room at will. Also, centers can be set outside the room, and small groups (or individuals) can leave the principal classroom on a rotating basis. There are many possibilities for using learning centers, and each teacher needs to apply them to his specific situation. Although each diagram contains a certain set of learning centers, these can be mixed up as long as the noise and time factors are considered.

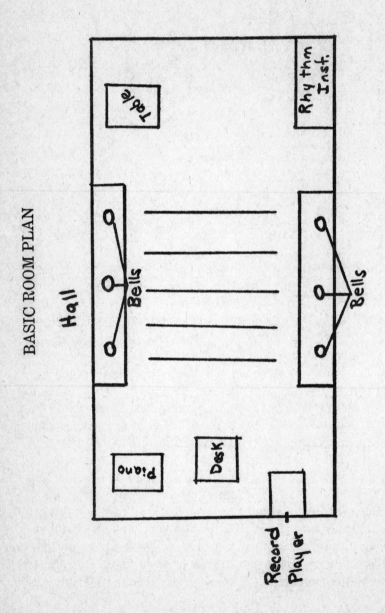

BASIC ROOM PLAN

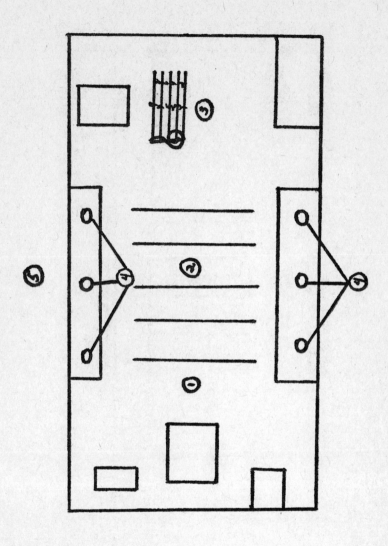

1. Rhythm Flash Cards.
2. Rhythm Flash Cards (Using Notes).
3. Note Toss.
4. Playing with Numbers.
5. Chord Accompaniments (Using bell chording).

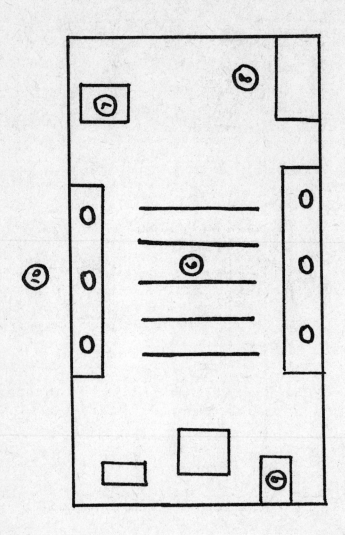

6. Musical Puzzles.
7. Matching Sounds.
8. Rhythm Bingo.
9. Listening Sheet.
10. Playing the Autoharp.

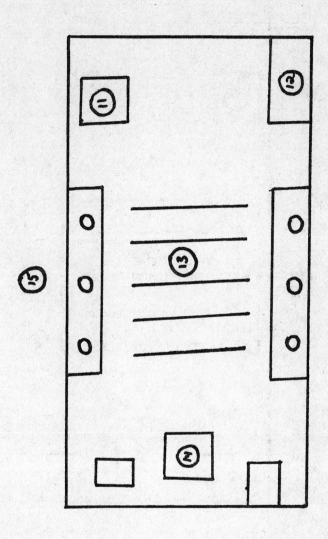

11. Creating an Oriental Accompaniment.
12. Performing an Oriental Accompaniment.
13. Clue Story.
14. Rhythm Game Board and Cards.
15. Bottle Playing.

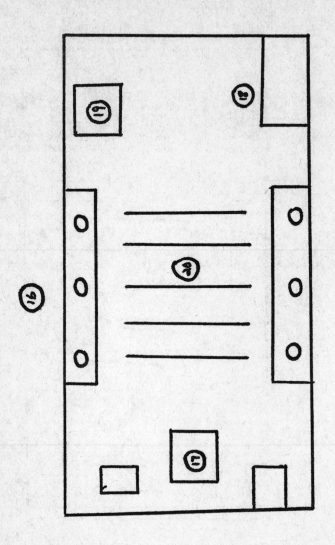

16. Matching Bell Tones.
17. Composer Card Game.
18. Playing the Recorder.
19. Creating a Major Composition.
20. Instrument Puzzle.

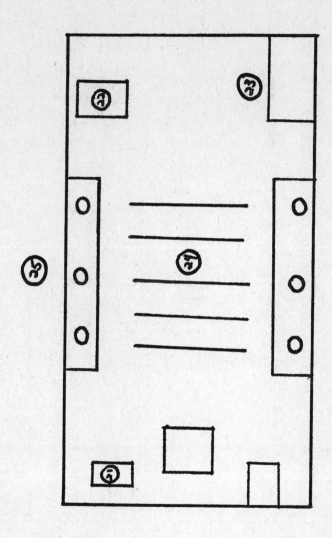

21. Partner Song Search.
22. Singing Puppets (Decide on Theme).
23. Singing Puppets (Perform Play).
24. Mathematical Rhythm.
25. Labeling Instruments.

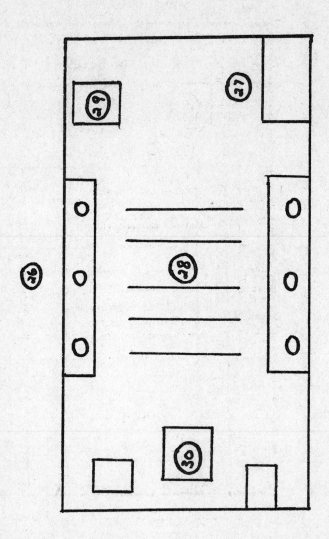

26. Identification of Instruments.
27. Musical Note Name Game.
28. Written Work Sheet.
29. Instrumental Families.
30. Mathematical Rhythm.

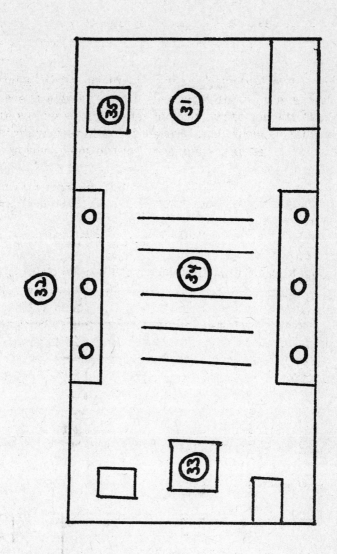

31. Creating Dances.
32. Playing Duets.
33. Form Shapes.
34. Information Hunt.
35. Supply the Mystery Word.

ADDITIONAL HELP AND EXTRA-CURRICULAR ACTIVITIES

In most self-contained music classrooms the teacher normally must adjust the progress of the class to the average students. Consequently, there are some students who find the work too easy and without a challenge. Usually there are a few other students who cannot learn as rapidly as the average student, and the work is too difficult for them. Both of these groups form special problems for the teacher and can often become discipline problems. In order to find additional activities for advanced students or extra reinforcement work for remedial students, the Learning Activities Section may be used. Such material may be organized in the form of a learning center, given as homework, or given as extra material during the regular class period. Although this requires extra time for the teacher, the task becomes easier by using the activities described throughout this book. It is well worth the time spent preparing these extra activities, considering the reduction of discipline problems and the improved results of the music classroom.

Because of interest in music and enjoyment from the regular music period, some students may seek extra-curricular activities in the area of music. The Activities Section will be helpful in setting up such extra-curricular activities. The teacher may plan special choruses, class lessons (piano, guitar, ukulele, percussion), small singing groups, music labs with learning centers, dance groups and lessons, or an area for special music games. Activities that are attractive and varied should provide additional musical learning for students, which in turn can benefit the entire music program.

LEARNING PACKETS

Learning packets can be made by referring to a specific area in the Activities Section and selecting activities to include in an individualized learning packet. Activities used in the packet should be those that students can use without a great deal of help from the teacher. Each student can work at his own pace, with the fast learners advancing to additional packets while slow learners take their time to complete a beginning packet. Each packet should include specific instructions and materials needed to complete the lessons. Students may hand in (for evaluation) papers included in the packet so that the teacher can keep posted on each student's progress. Packets can be made on any subject and the activities selected should meet the needs of a specific class. The contents of a typical packet are listed below for the purpose of teacher reference.

LEARNING ACTIVITIES PACKET: DYNAMICS IN MUSIC

Prerequisite Knowledge:

A child should have had some previous experience in listening.

Objectives:

1. Students will further their understanding of dynamics by labelling sounds as "soft" or "loud."

2. Students will further their knowledge of dynamics by matching Italian terms to letters.

3. Students will further their knowledge of dynamics by creating and playing melodies, using various dynamic levels.

4. Students will gain a better understanding of dynamics by associating animals with dynamic markings.

Materials Needed:

Tape Recorder

Dynamics Booklet

Crayons

Instruments

Teacher's Script for Tape

(When the tape begins, make various loud and soft sounds of different timbre.) This lesson is all about loud and soft sounds and how they can be used in music to make it more interesting when you listen. If all our music were the same volume, it would get pretty boring. Have you ever noticed that on TV the commercials are made louder than the television programs? They are louder to get your attention. At school if you are talking to your neighbor and the teacher wants your attention she will talk louder. Here is an example of how a composer named Haydn got the attention of his audience. (Play the theme of the *Surprise Symphony*). Did Haydn get your attention? Why do you suppose Haydn called his composition the *Surprise Symphony*? (pause) That's right. He put in a surprise to take up his audience. Now if you are ready find the "Dynamics" booklet.[13]

In Activity Number One you will find two examples. Put an X on the one that is making the loudest sound in each example and then check your answers which you will find on page two of the "Dynamics" booklet. (Record all the sounds for Activity Number One.)

Now you are ready for Activity Number Two. In this activity there are two examples given for each question. Put an "X" by the softest one and then check your answers on page two. (Record all the sounds for Activity Number Two).

In music you may see letters that stand for Italian words meaning soft or loud. "PP" stands for "pianissimo" and it means very soft. If you see "p" it stands for "piano," which in Italian means soft. "M" is used for "mezzo" (or medium), so "mp" means "mezzo piano" in Italian or "medium soft" in English. "F" means "forte" (or loud) so "mf" means to play or sing medium loud. If you see "ff" you should sing or play very loud ("fortissimo" in Italian). These terms are listed on page two of your booklet, so stop the tape and study them before proceeding.

Other methods of varying dynamic levels in music are the crescendo and decrescendo marks. Look at the

---

[13]Mila Williams, taken from a "Dynamics" packet prepared for elementary music where she teaches in Burlington, Iowa, p.1.

dynamic terms section on page two. The crescendo means to gradually get louder (turn volume of the radio up). The decrescendo means to gradually get softer (turn the volume of a radio down). Now turn to page one, Activity Three in your booklet. Match the letter to the Italian term and then write the English meaning beside it. The first item is completed for you. When you finish turn to page two to check your answers.

There are several ways that a composer can make the music crescendo or descrescendo. He can add voices for a crescendo (louder) or take voices away for a descrescendo (softer). Listen to this example of crescendo and decrescendo by adding or taking away voices. (Play examples of this method.) Can you think of another way? Yes, play the instruments or sing gradually louder or softer. (Play examples of this method.) Another way to create a crescendo or descrescendo is to start at a distance and move closer. When the music is far away it is soft and, as it comes closer, it gets louder. (Play a musical example of a train or parade.)

Now look at Activity Four on page three of your booklet. Play the C scale on the bells and crescendo going up and decrescendo going down. Listen as I play it and then rewind the tape and try it with me (record scale.)

Now that you know all about dynamics, create a soft melody on the bells and play it for the teacher or record it to be played later. This is Activity Five on page three of your booklet. For Activity Six, create a loud melody on the bells and play it.

Activity Seven page three. Use one of the techniques of crescendo and decrescendo (adding instruments or taking away instruments, gradually playing softer or louder, or starting far away and coming near) and create a song for the teacher to hear.

We could choose animals to represent different dynamic levels. A small quiet animal should represent the "pp" (pianissimo) and the animal could be bigger and louder until you select a very large loud animal to represent the "ff" (fortissimo). Turn to Activity Eight on

pages four to six and draw animals to represent each of
the dynamic markings.

The next activity involves listening to a recording
and outlining the dynamic levels. Use the proper letter
to represent each of the Italian words. You may need to
listen to the recording several times to be able to label
each section accurately. Refer to Activity Nine on page
seven to complete this activity. The form of the song is
outlined for you. Put the proper dynamic letter in each
space. (Record example to correspond to the form used
in the booklet. Make certain dynamic levels are obvious).

Now write a song on the staff paper for Activity Ten
on page seven, and include dynamic markings in your
song. Be sure you use the correct rhythms for the time
signature, 2/4. Hand the song in and I will play it for you
on the piano.

Now you know all about dynamics in music. They
help to make the music more interesting, so we should
use them to sing with expression.

DYNAMICS BOOKLET
STUDENT'S COPY

DYNAMICS BOOKLET
PAGE ONE

Activity One—Circle the item that makes the *loudest* sound.

1. Drum   Bell
2. Piano   Drum
3. Tambourine   Maraca
4. Whistle   Scream
5. Wind   Thunder

6. Tuba   Flute
7. Marimba   Piano
8. Solo   Choir
9. Stomping   Clapping
10. Band   Clarinet

Activity Two—Put an "X" beside the item that makes the *softest* sound.

1. Car   Truck
2. Triangle   Drum
3. Spanish Guitar
   Electric Guitar
4. Closing Door
   Slamming Door
5. Trumpet   Clarinet

6. Whispering   Shouting
7. Small Rocks   Large Rocks
8. Bells   Piano
9. Group Marching
   One Person Marching
10. Wood Block   Sand Blocks

Activity Three—Match the letter with the Italian term and then write the English meaning in the blank space.

1.	_soft_ p	Fortissimo
2.	___ f	Forte
3.	___ mp	Piano
4.	___ ff	Crescendo
5.	___	Mezzo Forte
6.	___ pp	Decrescendo
7.	___ mf	Pianissimo
8.	___	Mezzo Piano

DYNAMICS BOOKLET
PAGE TWO

Answers to Activity One

1.	Drum	6.	Tuba
2.	Piano	7.	Piano
3.	Tambourine	8.	Choir
4.	Scream	9.	Stomping
5.	Thunder	10.	Band

Answers to Activity Two

1.	Car	6.	Whispering
2.	Triangle	7.	Small Rocks
3.	Spanish Guitar	8.	Bells
4.	Closing Door	9.	One Person Marching
5.	Clarinet	10.	Sand Blocks

Dynamic Terms

Letter Symbol	Italian Term	English Meaning
pp	Pianissimo	Very Soft
p	Piano	Soft
mp	Mezzo Piano	Medium Soft
mf	Mezzo Forte	Medium Loud
f	Forte	Loud
ff	Fortissimo	Very Loud
	Crescendo	Gradually Get Louder
	Decrescendo	Gradually Get Softer

DYNAMICS BOOKLET

PAGE THREE

Activity Four—Play the C Scale on the bells and crescendo going up and decrescendo going down.

Activity Five—Create a soft melody on the bells and play it for the teacher, or record it to be played later.

Activity Six—Create a loud melody on the bells and play it for the teacher, or record it to be played later.

Activity Seven—Use one of the techniques of crescendo and decrescendo (adding instruments or taking away instruments, gradually playing softer or louder, or starting away and coming near) and create a song for the teacher to hear.

DYNAMICS BOOKLET

PAGE FOUR

Activity Eight—Draw and color animals to represent each of the
dynamic markings. Use small quiet animals for
the soft sounds and bigger and louder animals to
represent louder markings.

pp	Pianissimo	Very Soft

p	Piano	Soft

DYNAMICS BOOKLET
PAGE FIVE

| mp | Mezzo Piano | Medium Soft |

| mf | Mezzo Forte | Medium Loud |

DYNAMICS BOOKLET

PAGE SIX

f	Forte	Loud

ff	Fortissimo	Very Loud

DYNAMICS BOOKLET
PAGE SEVEN

Activity Nine—Listen to the recording and put the proper dynamic letter in each space.

Introduction   A   B   A   C   A

_____   ___   ___   ___   ___   ___

Activity Ten—Write a song on the staff paper and include dynamic markings in your song. Be sure you use the correct rhythms for the time signature.

Index

245

Index 249